The Poor and Their Money

The Poor and Their Money

Stuart Rutherford

OXFORD
UNIVERSITY PRESS

OXFORD
UNIVERSITY PRESS

YMCA Library Building, Jai Singh Road, New Delhi 110001

Oxford University Press is a department of the University of Oxford. It furthers the
University's objective of excellence in research, scholarship, and education
by publishing worldwide in

Oxford   New York

Athens   Auckland   Bangkok   Bogota   Buenos Aires   Calcutta
Cape Town   Chennai   Dar es Salaam   Delhi   Florence   Hong Kong   Istanbul
Karachi   Kuala Lumpur   Madrid   Melbourne   Mexico City   Mumbai
Nairobi   Paris   Sao Paolo   Singapore   Taipei   Tokyo   Toronto   Warsaw

with associated companies in Berlin Ibadan
Oxford is a registered trade mark of Oxford University Press
in the UK and in certain other countries

Published in India
By Oxford University Press, New Delhi

ISBN 019 565255 X

Typeset in 10 on 12 Times New Roman
by Inosoft Systems, New Delhi 110 092
Printed at Rashtriya Printers, Delhi 110 032
Published by Manzar Khan, Oxford University Press
YMCA Library Building, Jai Singh Road, New Delhi 110 001

Foreword

The UK government is committed to working with others to meet the internationally agreed targets for poverty reduction. These targets are both achievable and affordable. However we need the political will to deliver them, and we need the right policies and instruments in place to bring real benefits to the poor.

Microfinance—financial services for the poor—is one of these instruments. Department for International Development (DFID) has been actively involved in promoting the benefits of microfinance for nearly ten years, mainly in Sub-Saharan Africa and South Asia. Most of our support has gone through non-governmental organizations, which are particularly well positioned to reach a large number of poor people. This is achieved by bridging the often wide gap between the formal finanical sector and the informal or indigenous systems which exist in many countries.

The study of Stuart Rutherford, a microfinance practitioner with substantial experience of designing and managing microfinance programmes, shows the depth and range of systems that poor people themselves have established to manage their financial risks and needs. Rutherford demonstrates not only the reasons why poor people need financial services and the type of services they most value, but also, importantly for donors, how we can learn from them in promoting and providing microfinance.

Microfinance will continue to play an important role in meeting the challenges of eliminating poverty. This study provides an excellent insight into how best we can do this and deserves to be taken seriously by all those who work in this field.

January 2000

Clare Short, MP
Secretary of State (DFID)

Preface

This essay is about how poor people in developing countries manage their money. It describes how they handle their savings, from keeping bank notes under the floorboards to running sophisticated savings and loan clubs. It illustrates the variety of moneylenders and deposit collectors who serve the poor, including the new micro-finance institutions (MFIs)—semi-formal or formal banks that specialize in working with poor clients.

The essay illustrates the principles that underlie these phenomena, and I hope it will stimulate those who would like to improve the quality of financial services that are offered to the poor. Essentially, it is about how a better understanding of financial services for the poor can lead to better provision of such services.

The audience I have in mind is composed mainly of those who provide or promote financial services for the poor, and their backers. I am thinking of people who work for MFIs and non-government organizations (NGOs), aid donors, and banks and co-operatives who want to reach the poor. I hope, too, that some members of the general public will find the essay interesting and readable.

The essay therefore aims at clarity. I have tried to avoid jargon. I have included a bibliography that has been annotated to help practitioners. Most of the cases that I use to illustrate my points are ones that I have personally investigated during more than twenty years of research and practice in the subject on three continents (though there is a strong bias towards Asia, where I have lived and worked for fifteen years). *The Poor and Their Money* is *not* an 'academic' paper. I hope some academics will read the essay, because they too influence the growing 'microfinance industry', but they should not expect it to conform to academic standards of presentation and argument. The statements I have made are grounded on my long-standing interest and experience in the field, and above all on my conversations with poor people about how they actually use financial services. I have not made any assumptions that are not based on this kind of experience. but in the interest of brevity and readability I have not quoted chapter-and-verse in support of all my arguments, as would be required in a formal academic paper. I invite academics to get in touch with me (at safesave@aol.com) if they would like more references, or if they would like to challenge or amplify what I have written.

Nor is the essay intended as a 'manual'. I do not provide step-by-step guidance to set up an MFI. Although I describe my own work—the MFI called *Safe*Save that features at the end of Chapter Two—I do not for one minute think that *Safe*Save is the last word in financial services for the poor. *Safe*Save is included in the essay to illustrate some important issues, and *not* as a recommended 'recipe'. Indeed, by the time you read this, *Safe*Save should have moved on to new and—we hope—better products. *Safe*Save happens to be my 'action research' project.

The 'microfinance industry' is in its adolescence. There have been encouraging breakthroughs in the last two or three decades— as Chapter Three shows. But the potential for growth and improvement is huge. There are still millions of poor people to reach, and hundreds of new ways of reaching them waiting to be discovered and developed. I hope this essay will accelerate this voyage of discovery.

A version of chapters one and two of the essay circulated on the internet from early 1998. An earlier version of the complete essay was published in February 1999 by the Finance and Development Research Programme at the Institute for Development Policy and Management, University of Manchester, as 'The Poor and Their Money', *Working Paper Number 3*.

December 1999   Dhaka, Bangladesh

Acknowledgements

I was persuaded to write this essay by Sukhwinder Singh Arora at DFID, Delhi. Much of the material I use was uncovered in his company in cities around India in the course of work for DFID. To him I owe a double vote of thanks. Graham Wright, now working for DFID and UNDP in East Africa, tramped through villages with me in Bangladesh and the Philippines and provided great encouragement. My assistant S.K. Sinha was closely involved in researching material. Assistance has come from many sources including the many organizations with whom I have worked. Although too many to list, I would like to specifically mention ASA, ActionAid (especially in Bangladesh and Vietnam), BURO Tangail, CARE International (in several countries), DFID, and PLAN International, as well as my own MFI *Safe*Save. My academic institution, the Institute for Development Policy and Management (IDPM) at the University of Manchester, and the Microfinance Training Programme at the Economics Institute in Boulder, Colorado, where I have taught, provided opportunities to discuss and develop my ideas. Those who have helped through commentary on drafts of this essay (or parts of it) are many, and include Edward Abbey, Dale Adams, Theirry Van Basterlaer, Warren Brown, Greg Chen, Bob Christen, Robert Christie, Hege Gulli, Robert Hickson, David Hulme, Feisal Hussain, Sanae Ito, Susan Johnson, Leonard Mutesasire, Vijay Mahajan, Mohini Malhotra, Imran Matin, Jonathan Morduch, Marguerite Robinson, Rich Rosenberg, Hans Seibel, William Steel, Astrid Ursem and David Wright. I have benefited from all of them, and while I am willing to share the credit for any virtues of this essay, I jealously guard sole ownership of its faults.

Thousands of users and would-be users of financial services for the poor around the world have given their time to teach me how and why the existence and quality of financial services is important to them. Since it is hard to list or thank them, I acknowledge my debt by dedicating this essay to them.

Contents

List of Figures

1

The Need to Save

Although their incomes may be tiny or irregular, there are many times when poor people need sums of money that are bigger than what they have in hand. The need for these 'usefully large lump sums' arises from life-cycle events such as birth, education, marriage, and death, from emergency situations, and from the discovery of opportunities to make investments in assets or businesses. The only reliable and sustainable way that they can obtain these sums is to build them, somehow or other, from their savings. So poor people have to save, and financial services for the poor are there to help them find ways to do so.

THE POOR AS SAVERS

The poor want to save, and do save... but it is not easy

A popular and useful definition of a poor person is someone who does not have much money. Among academics, and in the aid industry, this definition has gone out of fashion. But it suits my present purposes well, so I shall stick to it. In this essay, when I talk about 'the poor', I mean people who, compared to their fellow citizens, don't have much money.

If you do not have much money it is especially important that you manage well what money you have. Poor people are at a disadvantage here, because the banks and insurance companies and other financial institutions that serve the better-off rarely cater to the poor. Nevertheless, poor people do seek and find a wide variety of ways of managing their money, as examples in this essay will show. The essay argues that we can learn a lot from the more successful money-managing efforts of the poor, and use that learning to design new and better ways of bringing banking services to the slums and villages of the developing world.

Choosing to Save...

Managing money well begins with hanging on to what you have. This means avoiding unnecessary expenditure and then finding a safe place to store whatever money is left over. Making that choice— *the choice to save rather than to consume*—is the foundation of money management.

...But Finding it Hard to Do So

Poor people run into problems with money management at this very first hurdle. If you live in an urban slum or in a straw hut in a village, finding a safe place to store savings is not easy. Bank notes tucked into rafters, buried in the earth, rolled inside hollowed-out bamboo, or thrust into clay piggy banks, can be lost or stolen or blown away or may just rot. Certainly their value will decline, because of inflation. But the physical risks may be the least of the problem. Much tougher is keeping the cash safe from the many claims on it—claims by relatives who have fallen on hard times, by importunate neighbours, by hungry or sick children or alcoholic husbands, by your mother-in-law (who knows you have that secret hoard somewhere)[1] and by landlords, creditors and beggars. Finally, even when you do have a little cash left over at the day's end, if you do not have somewhere safe to put it you will most probably spend it in some trivial way or other. I have lost count of the number of women who have told me how hard it is to save at home, and how much they would value a safe, simple way to save.

Nevertheless, the poor *can* save, *do* save, and *want* to save money. Only those so poor that they have left the cash economy altogether— elderly disabled widows and widowers for example, who live by begging food from neighbours—cannot save money. This essay is not about them.

Can the Poor Really Save?

The fact that the poor want to save and have some capacity to save is not self-evident. If you do not know much about how the poor actually organize their lives you may assume that the poor 'are too poor to save'. The poor spend all their income and still do not get

---

[1] In several languages there are special words for that small hidden sum of cash that a woman will try to keep secret from her men-folk. For example, in the slums of Dhaka women use the Bengali word 'jula'.

enough to eat, so how can they save? The poor may need loans, but the last thing they need, you may think, is a savings service.

Ins and Outs

By the time you have finished this essay you will see that this is a misconception. But for the time being, notice that people (and not just the poor) may save money whilst most of it goes *out* (like keeping a few coins back from the housekeeping money) as well as when it comes in (deducting savings at source from your wage or other income). Even the poorest have to spend money to buy basic items like food and fuel, and each time they do so there is the opportunity to save something, however tiny. Many poor housewives try to save in this way, even if their working husbands fail to save anything from their income.

That the poor do succeed in saving something is shown by their habit of lending each other small amounts of money (as well as small amounts of rice or kerosene or salt). In this 'reciprocal lending' I lend you a few cents today on the understanding that you'll do the same for me at some other time. This practice is so common that such loans form the bulk of financial transactions that poor people get involved in, even if the amounts involved add up to only a small proportion of the total value in circulation through financial services for the poor. The practice depends entirely on the poor's capacity and willingness to save.

This essay is about saving *money*. People save in other ways, of course, and we shall take that into account, briefly, in the notes at the end of this chapter. But for the time being I want to pursue my basic message in the simplest way, and that means concentrating on money savings. The poor, we have claimed, can and do save. But why do they do so?

THE POOR AS BIG SPENDERS

The poor need, surprisingly often, to spend large sums of money

You may not yet be fully convinced that the poor can and do (and want to) save. So we shall move on to the spending needs of the poor, which are less controversial.

The Need to Spend

Just because you are poor does not mean that all your expenditure will be in small sums. Much of it may be—you may buy only a little food or clothing at a time. But from time to time you need to spend large sums. How we classify these needs is a matter of choice: I like to list them under three main categories, 'life-cycle' events, emergency needs, and investment opportunities.

Life-cycle needs: In Bangladesh and India, the dowry system makes marrying daughters an expensive business. In parts of Africa, burying deceased parents can be very costly. These are just two examples of 'life-cycle' events for which the poor need to amass large lump sums. Other such events include childbirth, education, home-building, widowhood and old-age generally, and the desire to bequeath lump sum to their heirs. Then there are the recurrent festivals like Eid, Christmas, or Diwali. In each case the poor need to be able to get their hands on sums of money which are much bigger than the amounts of cash which are normally found in the household. Many of these needs can be anticipated, even if their exact date is unknown. The awareness that such outlays are looming on the horizon is a source of great anxiety for many poor people.

Emergencies: Emergencies that create a sudden and unanticipated need for a large sum of money come in two forms—personal and impersonal. Personal emergencies include sickness or injury, the death of a bread-winner or the loss of employment, and theft or harassment. Impersonal ones include events such as war, floods, fires, cyclones, and—for slum dwellers—the bulldozing of their homes by the authorities. Again, you will be able to think of other examples. Each creates a sudden need for more cash than can normally be found at home. Finding a way to insure themselves against such troubles would help millions of poor people.

Investment opportunities: Besides innumerable *needs* for spending large sums of cash, there are *opportunities* to do so. There may be opportunities to invest in an existing or new business, or to buy land or other productive assets. The lives of some poor people can be transformed if they can afford to pay a bribe to get a permanent job (often in government service). The poor, like all of us, also like to invest in costly items that make life more comfortable—better roofing, better furniture, a water-pump, a fan, a television. One of these investment opportunities—setting up a new business or expanding an existing one—has recently attracted a lot of attention from the aid industry and from the new generation of banks that work with the poor. But business investment is in fact just one of many needs and opportunities that require the poor to become occasional 'big spenders'.

FINANCIAL SERVICES FOR POOR PEOPLE

In this essay, we shall be concentrating on how the poor obtain the large lump sums they need from time to time. We shall be reviewing the financial services—formal and informal—that have evolved to serve this need. These are services that are urgently and frequently needed for the vast majority of poor people, for the reasons set out in the previous section. They are the ones discussed in this essay.

Of course, there are other services used by the poor that are 'financial' in the wider sense, such as those that ease the transmission or conversion of currency. Examples are sending money home from town or abroad. Apart from this brief mention, these services (important though they are to many poor people) are not dealt with in this essay.

So, to return to our main question: how are the poor to get hold of the large lump sums they so often need? They might be lucky and have cash gifted to them, or be in some other way the beneficiary of charity—but this can hardly be relied on. It is not a sustainable way of getting access to large sums.

Three common ways of raising large sums are:

- selling assets they already hold (or expect to hold).
- mortgaging (or 'pawning') those assets.
- finding a way of turning their many small savings into large lump sums.

Stocks and Flows

The *first method* listed above—the sale of assets—is usually a straightforward matter that doesn't ordinarily require any 'financial' services. However, poor people sometimes sell, in advance, assets that they don't hold now but expect to hold in the future. The most common rural example is the advance sale of crops. These 'advances' are a form of financing, since the buyer provides, in effect, a loan that will be repaid from the yet-to-be harvested crop. The advance may be spent on financing the farming costs required to produce that crop. But they may just as likely be used on any of the other needs and opportunities we reviewed in the previous section, or simply on surviving until harvest time.

The *second method*—mortgage and pawn—enables poor people to convert assets into cash and back again. It is the chance (not always realized) to regain the asset that distinguishes this second method from the first. As in the straightforward sale of assets, such services require the user to have a stock of wealth in the form of an asset of some sort. They allow the user to exploit their ownership of this stock of wealth by transforming it temporarily into cash. The most common examples are the pawning in shops in towns and the mortgaging of land in the countryside.

These first two methods require the users to have assets, and poor people, almost by definition, have very few assets. This fact severely limits the effectiveness of these two methods. It makes them neither reliable nor sustainable. Only the third method is free of this limitation.

The *third method* enables poor people to convert their small savings into lump sums. This requires the users to have a flow of savings, however small or irregular. It allows them to exploit their capacity to make savings by offering a variety of mechanisms by which these savings can be transformed into lump sums. These three are at the heart of all financial services for the poor, whether they are informal or formal, large or small.

A set of simple diagrams will make this clearer, I hope, so, proceed to introduce the basic system of diagrams that I use throughout this essay. In these diagrams, time is represented by the horizontal axis, and value (of money) by the vertical axis.

Saving up: 'Saving up' is the most obvious way to convert savings into lump sums. It allows a lump sum to be enjoyed in future in exchange for a series of savings made now. Many poor people prefer this mechanism because it produces an 'unencumbered' lump sum—it is yours to do what you like with once you've built it up. But as we have seen, the poor find it hard to find a safe place to keep their savings.

In Figure 1.1, savings made by the user are shown as negative values (below the horizontal line) since they are saved (deducted) from the user's expenditure, and the saved-up sum is shown as a positive value when it is 'withdrawn' and becomes available to be spent. Note that as soon as a sum is 'withdrawn' most savers like to start saving all over again: the diagram shows this is as two further saved sums on the right hand side of the withdrawal.

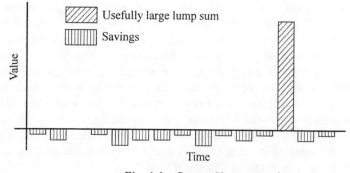

Fig. 1.1 *Saving Up*

Saving down: Another way to turn exactly the same series of savings into a lump sum is to get someone to give you the lump sum *first*, as a loan, and then use the savings to repay the loan over time. Such loans can be thought of as 'advances against future savings'. This is what I call 'saving down'(Figure 1.2)—since it is the exact opposite of saving up. But just as the poor find it hard to find a safe place to save up, many of them also find it very hard to find someone to help them 'save down'. Indeed, the most common complaint about moneylenders in developing countries is not that they charge extortionate rates of interest (though some do, of course), but that they are simply not available. As an Indian proverb has it, 'a good village is one with a good well and a good moneylender'.

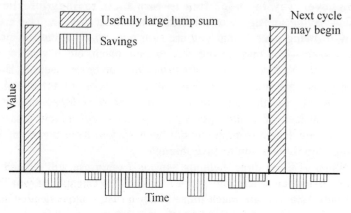

Fig. 1.2 *Saving Down*

Saving through: Finally we come to 'saving through', as shown in Figure 1.3 in which the saver goes on making a more or less continuous stream of savings that get converted to a lump sum at some intermediate point in time. Insurance policies do this—when you insure your car you make a series of savings (monthly premiums or whatever) and take lump sums back each time you crash into the gatepost and need to repair the bodywork. Not many poor people are insured—though many would dearly like to be—but other 'saving through' mechanisms are popular among them. They take the form of savings clubs of one sort or another and we shall look at them in detail in Chapter Three.

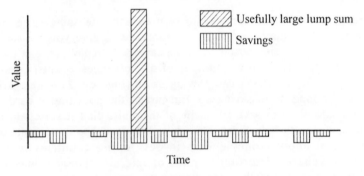

Fig. 1.3   *Saving Through*

No Choice But to Save...In Whatever Available Way

Whichever way the poor find to turn their savings into lump sums—saving up, down or through—they *have to* save. The great irony of being poor is that you are 'too poor to save, but too poor not to save'—you may not be able to save much, but if you do not save at all you have no way of getting hold of those 'usefully large lump sums' that you so often need. When the poor are not saving, it is rarely the case that they do not want or need to. More often it is due to the lack of a safe opportunity to save—no reliable place to save up, no friendly moneylender to help you save down, or no saving club to help you to save through.

Which of these three methods you most often use will depend to a large extent on where you happen to live. For example, if you live in South Asia you are much more likely to use a moneylender than if you live in East Africa, where there are not many moneylenders serving the poor. East Africa doesn't have many deposit collectors, either, whereas in many countries of West Africa they are very common. All these three regions have many savings clubs which allow the poor to 'save through', but the East African poor have to rely on them more than the poor of South Asia and West Africa. The fact that South Asians will probably be 'saving down', whereas West Africans are more likely to be 'saving 'up' and East Africans 'saving through' is another fact that has led me to believe that moneylending, deposit collecting and savings clubs are devices that may look very different but are in fact all essentially doing the same job—the job of helping poor people turn their savings into usefully large lump sums.

Basic Personal Financial Intermediation

The set of mechanisms I call saving up, down and through need a name that is less clumsy than 'services which enable poor people to convert their small savings into usefully large lump sums'. I suggest the term 'basic personal financial intermediation'. I admit this is still a mouthful, but it does describe the process at work.

The process is one of 'financial intermediation' of the kind that a regular banker would recognize,[2] because many small savings are 'intermediated' ('carried across') into lump sums. But the process is 'personal' because we are talking about how one poor person can turn her savings into a lump sum for her own use (whereas bankers normally talk about intermediating the savings of many into loans for a few—who may be entirely different people). Finally I call the process 'basic' because it a basic requirement of everyday life for most poor people.

ORGANIZATION OF THE ESSAY

This introductory chapter has laid out the basic argument of the essay.

The second chapter illustrates 'saving up, saving down and saving through' by means of actual examples from the slums and villages of the developing world.

[2] *The Economist* defines a financial intermediary as 'any individual or institution that mediates between savers (that is sources of funds) and borrowers (that is users of funds).' *Pocket Finance*, Economist Books, London, 1994, page 94.

Chapters Three and Four are devoted to detailed descriptions of the various kinds of informal financial services for the poor, while Chapter Five takes a look at microfinance institutions—the new banks that are learning the way to provide banking services for poor people.

The last chapter, Chapter Six, reflects on what we have learned, and suggests some principles that we should keep in mind when planning better financial services for the poor.

Finally, a reading list, arranged by chapter, and annotated, provides suggestions for further reading.

Box 1.1   Financial Services for Poor People

Financial services for poor people exist to help them get hold of usefully large sums of cash on the many occasions when they *need* the cash or have an *opportunity* to invest it.

Assets *(stocks)* can be sold to raise cash, but this method is limited by the fact that the poor hold few assets.

Mortgaging or pawning assets (exchanging them temporarily for cash) is an important financial service for the poor, but once again it is limited by the poors' lack of assets.

The only reliable and sustainable way of raising lump sums of cash is to find a way of building them from one's capacity to save small amounts from time to time, here referred to as basic personal financial intermediation which may involve:

- Saving up: where you accumulate savings *first* and take the resulting lump sum *later;*
- Saving down: where you take the lump sum *first* as an advance (or loan) against future savings;
- Saving through: where you take a lump sum *at the time it is needed* in exchange for a continuous stream of savings; or
- some combination of all three.

In each case, saving is the essential ingredient, and the devices and services are the ways of converting savings into usefully large lump sums.

That is why the poor need to save.

NOTES

Town and country. We noted that people can save money when it is 'on the way out' (during expenditure) as well as when it is on the way in (at the time income is received). This helps to correct a common misconception about the differences between town and country. I sometimes hear it is said that 'in the urban slums people can save because they have a variety of sources continually producing income—but rural farmers may only get income at the end of each growing season, and that is the only time they can save'. This ignores the fact that in many countries the rural poor are often not farmers, since they have lost their land. They are labourers and may earn on a daily or weekly basis. But even those poor who are farmers go to market frequently—once or twice a month, or even weekly—to buy perishable or expendable items like salt, fresh food, kerosene oil, matches, and so on. The money they use for this can come from several sources, including the sale of short-term farm produce like eggs, chickens, or fruit, or from income from supplementary work like cutting firewood, or selling bigger items in which they have stored (or saved) value, such as stocks of grain, pigs or goats. Each such market visit presents an opportunity to save money, even if this saving simply converts a non-money form of saving (the piglet) into cash savings.

Saving in kind. Mentioning piglets reminds us that poor people often save in kind. These non-monetary savings may be very important to their owners, but they are not the subject of this essay, except in the following sense. Poor people sometimes store their savings in livestock or other non-money ways simply because they do not have access to a safe, rewarding, inflation-proof means to save money. Once they are given the opportunity, poor people often choose to convert some of their non-money savings into cash savings. This is because cash savings can be more useful, and less risky, than non-money savings. The piglet may get sick and die or be stolen, and if all that you need is two dollars to buy medicine for a sick child, it is rather troublesome to have to sell a piglet worth thirty dollars.[3] Also, non-money savings are themselves easier to manage if you have access to a cash-savings service. When you have sold the thirty-dollar piglet you need somewhere to put the twenty-eight dollars left over after buying the medicine. And if you save in the form of gold ornaments, as some poor people do, how did you save up the cash to buy the ornament in the first place? *Safe*Save customers often use *Safe*Save to save up enough to buy an ear-ring. The inescapable conclusion is this—that a cash-savings service is useful even to people who prefer to store most of their savings in non-cash

---

[3] Money is 'fungible'—it can be quickly converted into services or goods (including medicine and piglets). It is the point of money to be fungible. That's why we invented it.

forms. As the world becomes ever more monetized many poor people are coming to see that for themselves, and the demand for financial services grows.

Pawning. In some countries pawnshops have been outlawed, sometimes so successfully that some readers from those countries require an explanation of pawning (after which they normally recognize the phenomenon which tends to exist in their 'grey' economies under some local name). A pawn is a movable asset (most commonly a precious metal, above all gold) that it taken as security for a loan by a lender—the 'pawnbroker'.[4] You take your gold ring along to him and he weighs it and gives you, if you're lucky, about 60 per cent of its market value. When you pay him back (with interest) you get the ring back. If you never pay him back he keeps the ring and in the end sells it. Pawning is to the town what mortgaging land is to the countryside—an example of a class of financial services for the poor by which assets can be turned into cash and back again.

Other ways to get hold of usefully large sums of money. We noted that you can sometimes sell assets that you expect to hold in the future—selling your chickens before they have hatched, as it were. As well as selling assets like crops in advance, you can also sell your labour (or that of your children or spouse) in advance. This is common in rural Bangladesh and in several other countries. We could list other examples of ingenious ways to get hold of money, but this essay discusses those that are common everywhere, and which involve mainly financial transactions, rather than sales of goods or labour.

---

[4] This definition of pawning is similar to the conventional one for mortgaging. Another way to look at pawning is to say that it is not part of a loan contract, but is the sale of goods linked to a promise to buy it back again, under which part of its value is forfeited if the re-purchase fails to take place.

2

Three Ways to Save

There are several devices and services that allow the poor to save up, save down, or save through. But they are unevenly distributed across or within nations and populations, and many poor people have little access to them. As a result, they are in high demand, and the poor are prepared to pay high prices or to accept high levels of risk to get them, or to put a lot of effort into organizing them for themselves.

Of the propositions that were put forward in the first chapter, the ones that people usually find most strange are the ideas that:

- most poor people want to save, can save, and do save; and
- loans are often nothing more than a way of turning savings into lump sums

This chapter is devoted to a small number of examples of 'basic personal financial intermediation' that will, I hope, make these ideas feel less odd. Each example is true since I have personally investigated by observing and talking to the people involved. Each example, except the last, is typical of phenomena that are widespread among the poor all over the developing world—though of course the detail will vary from place to place.

SAVING UP: DEPOSIT COLLECTORS

The need to find a safe place to keep savings is so strong that some poor people willingly pay others to take their savings out of their hands and store them

We begin with 'saving up', and we start our journey in India, in the slums of the south-eastern town of Vijayawada. There I found Jyothi doing her rounds. Jyothi is a middle-aged semi-educated woman who makes her living as a peripatetic (wandering) deposit collector. Her clients are slum dwellers, mostly women. Jyothi has, over the years, built a good reputation as a safe pair of hands that can be trusted to take care of the savings of her clients.

This is how she works. She gives each of her clients a simple card, divided into 220 cells (eleven rows and twenty columns), as shown here. In each cell, clients commit themselves to saving a certain amount in a certain period. For example, one client may agree to save Rs 5 per cell, at the rate of one cell a day. This means that at the end of 220 days (since there are 220 cells) she will have deposited 220 times Rs 5, or Rs 1,100 (that's about $25 US). Having made this agreement, it is now Jyothi's duty to visit this client each day to collect the five rupees. In the card reproduced here the client has got as far as saving 47 times, for a total of Rs 235 to date.

JYOTHI'S SAVINGS

5	5	5	5	5	5	5	5	5	5	5	5	5	5	5	5	5	5	5	5
5	5	5	5	5	5	5	5	5	5	5	5	5	5	5	5	5	5	5	5
5	5	5	5	5	5	5													

When the contract is fulfilled—that is when the client has saved Rs 5, 220 times (which may actually take more or less than 220 days, because slum dwelling women are human beings and not slot machines), the client takes her savings back. However, she does not get it all back, since Jyothi has to be paid for the service she provides. These fees vary, but in Jyothi's case it is 20 out of the 220 cells—or Rs 100 out of the Rs 1,100 saved by the client in our example.

We can calculate Jyothi's fee as a percentage of the cash she handles. Her fee, at Rs 100 in Rs 1,100, can be said to be 9 per cent. Or, we can look at it in another way and work out the interest that her savers are earning on their savings. Obviously, since they get back *less* than they put in, they are earning a *negative* interest rate, but what is that rate? In the example given, it works out at about minus 30 per cent a year (see Box 2.1).

Box 2.1   Calculating Interest Rates for a 1 eposit Collector

In our example the client has saved Rs 1,100 over 220 days. This means that *on an average* over the 220-day period she had half that amount, or Rs 550, deposited with Jyothi. On that Rs 550 she has paid an interest of Rs 100, or 18 per cent over a 220-day period. Interest percentages are best calculated at an annual rate, so that it is easy to compare one rate with another. 18 per cent over 220 days is the same as 30 per cent over 365 days. So the *annual percentage rate* (APR) is about 30 per cent. In other words, the client is 'earning' interest at *minus* 30 per cent APR.

Why should savers be prepared to accept a negative interest rate on savings? We can give two answers, which complement each other. One response comes from economists. They would say 'these rates are so abnormal that there is obviously an imperfect market here'. They mean that the *demand* for savings services is not being freely matched by the *supply* of savings services. That is exactly correct in the Vijayawada slums. Apart from depending on people like Jyothi, slum dwellers have very few places to put their savings. Banks are too remote, physically and socially, and do not like to accept tiny deposits such as Rs 5 a day. It is extremely hard to save at home, as we noted in the first chapter. Competitors for Jyothi are few, because it takes a long time and a special sort of person to build up the reputation for safety that Jyothi has.

The second answer comes from the users of this system, and sheds light on the nature of their 'demand' for savings services. The first client I talked to was doing it to buy school fees and clothing for her two school-going children. She knew she would need about Rs 800 in early July, or miss out on admitting her children to school. Her husband, a day labourer, could not be relied on to come up with so much money at one time, and in any case he felt that looking after the children's education was *her* duty, not his. She knew she would not be able to save so large an amount at home—with so many more immediate demands on the scarce cash. I asked her if she understood that she was paying 30 per cent a year for the privilege of saving up with Jyothi. She said that she did, and still thought it a good bargain. Without Jyothi, she would not be able to school the children. Other users told similar stories, and slum dwellers in a neighbouring slum where there is no Jyothi at work actually envied Jyothi's clients.

In terms of the concept of basic personal financial intermediation, we can say that Jyothi's clients commit themselves to a series of equal and (more or less) regular but tiny *savings* which Jyothi holds for them until they are transformed (intermediated) into a usefully large lump sum (large enough to pay the school costs, for example). We can represent Jyothi's service by using a diagram of the type described in the first chapter. Obviously, Jyothi offers a *saving up* service, but we need to modify the 'saving up' diagram to take account of two things: the fee (or interest) that Jyothi charges, and the fact that she accepts equal (not unequal) deposit sizes.

Jyothi's savings are shown in Figure 2.1. We can show the savings and the fees below the horizontal axis, as negative values, since the client pays these *in* to Jyothi, and the lump sum above the axis, as a positive value, since the client gets this *out* of the system.

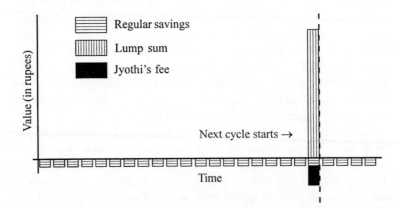

Fig. 2.1   *Jyothi's Savings*

Note one more thing about services like Jyothi's: clients often start a second cycle as soon as the first cycle is finished. That is why the broken vertical line after the pay-out, indicates the end of one cycle and the beginning of the next.

Box 2.2   Summing Up Jyothi's Savings

The market for savings deposits in slums is 'imperfect' (demand is not matched by supply).

Slum dwellers want to turn their savings into lump sums for many different needs and opportunities.

Unable to save at home, and unable to go to remote unfriendly banks, they trust their savings to unlicensed informal peripatetic collectors.

When they find one whom they can trust, time and time again, they are willing to pay a high price (as much as 30 per cent a year) to have that collector take away their savings and store them safely until needed.

The service that these deposit collectors render represents the most simple version of basic personal financial intermediation for poor people.

We look next at one of Jyothi's competitor—the urban money-lender.

SAVING DOWN: THE URBAN MONEYLENDER

In an environment where the demand for savings services far outstrips supply, it is not surprising that many loans to poor people turn out to be just another way of turning savings into lump sums—through the mechanism I call 'saving down'.

There are many kinds of moneylenders. There is one kind that is common in many urban slums of the sort where deposit collectors like Jyothi work. Indeed, I have taken my example from Vijayawada again because I want to draw a direct comparison with Jyothi. I got to know this moneylender's clients in a slum not far from the one where Jyothi works.

His working method is simple. He gives loans to poor people without any security (or 'collateral'), and then takes back his money in regular instalments over the next few weeks or months. He charges for this service by deducting a percentage (in his case 15 per cent) of the value of the loan at the time of disbursal. One of his clients reported the deal to me as follows.

'I run a very small shop' (it's a small timber box on stilts on the sidewalk inside which he squats and sells a few basic household goods) 'and I need the moneylender to help me maintain my stock of goods. I borrow Rs 1,000 from him from which he deducts Rs 150 as interest. He then visits me weekly and I repay the Rs 1,000 over ten weeks, at Rs 100 a week. As soon as I have paid him off he normally lets me have another loan.'

This client (Ramalu) showed me the scruffy bit of card that the moneylender had given him and on which his weekly repayments are recorded. It was quite like the cards Jyothi hands out. There are many other similarities between Jyothi and the moneylender. We can see that if we redraw our diagram as in Figure 2.2 to show this moneylender's system.

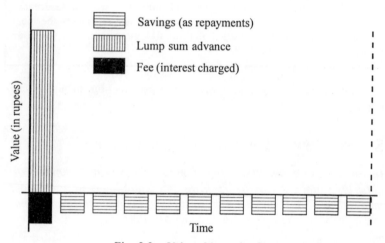

Fig. 2.2   *Urban Money-lenders*

The main difference—the fact that the pay-out comes first, as a loan, is immediately apparent. But let us look at the similarities. In each case the client is using the service to swap a series of small regular pay-ins (or savings) for a usefully big pay-out. In other words, these are both forms of basic personal financial inter-mediation. With the urban moneylender, the pay-out comes first, and can be understood as an *advance against future savings*. Indeed, very many loans to poor people are actually advances against savings, as we shall see.

Another similarity is that clients often proceed straight into a second cycle—and then a third and so on. When one has done several cycles it does not make much difference whether, in the *first* cycle, the loan or the savings came first—one may not even be able to remember. Every day (or week or month) a small *pay-in* is made and every now and then (every 220 days or every ten weeks) a usefully big *pay-out*. This is just what the poor need, as we saw earlier in the chapter. This is the essence of basic personal financial intermediation.

As in all cases of basic personal financial intermediation, the size of the pay-out is directly linked to the size of the pay-ins. In the case of Jyothi, the client makes the decision, by choosing the size of the pay-in. In the case of the moneylender, the moneylender makes the decision, by choosing the size of the loan (or at least its *maximum* size). To do this, he has to judge the client's capacity to save, and in this he is often helped by a history of previous similar deals with the same client or with people in similar situations.

Box 2.3   Calculating Interest Rates for an Urban Moneylender

For ten weeks the client had an average loan in his pocket of Rs 425. On that he paid Rs 150 interest, or about 35 per cent, for ten weeks. At a yearly rate (52 weeks) we divide 35 per cent by 10 and multiply by 52 to arrive at 180 per cent.

This brings us to another important difference, the difference in the price of the two services. The moneylender is more expensive. Calculating his rates in the same way as we calculated Jyothi's, we can see that the moneylender charges 15 per cent of the cash he handles (as opposed to Jyothi's 9 per cent), and charges an APR of around 180 per cent (as opposed to Jyothi's 30 per cent).

The client pays the moneylender more but of course the client gets more for his (or her) money. For one thing, the moneylender accepts the risk that the client may be unable or unwilling to make the pay-ins, a risk which Jyothi doesn't face (indeed, her clients have to accept the risk that *she will* run off with *their* money). Secondly, the moneylender puts up the initial finance for the first cycle, whereas Jyothi needs no capital to run her business. Thirdly, the moneylender has to use his judgement about the size of each contract, while Jyothi can happily leave that to her clients. For all these reasons clients pay the moneylender more than Jyothi for an essentially similar basic personal financial intermediation service. We can now see why the women in the slum next to Jyothi's envied Jyothi's clients their access to a safe and relatively cheap way to build a lump sum from their savings.

SAVING THROUGH: THE MERRY-GO-ROUND

But both sets of clients—Jyothi's and the moneylender's—could run the same sort of service for themselves, for free. To see how, we need to look at *RO*tating *Sa*vings and *C*redit *A*ssociations, or ROSCAs—a 'saving through' device. Since there are many kinds of ROSCAs we will look at a very simple one in this chapter, the 'merry-go-round' as it is practised in the slums of Nairobi, Kenya.

Mary, a woman whose ROSCA I studied there, is, like Ramalu, a very small vendor. She sells vegetables from a shelf set in the window of her hut. She is a member of a merry-go-round that has fifteen members, including herself. This is what they do.

Every day, day-in day-out, each of them saves 100 shillings. So each day a total of 1,500 shillings (about $40) is saved. Each day one of the fifteen women takes the full 1,500 shillings. After each of the fifteen women has taken the 'prize' in turn—which takes fifteen days of course—the cycle starts again. Mary was 'serial number 7' in the cycle. So seven days after the start of the first cycle, and then every fifteen days, she gets 1,500 shillings in return for 100 shillings put in every day. Mary told me she had been in this merry-go-round with the same fellow-members for two and a half years.

Figure 2.3 shows Mary's merry-go-round where the 'basic personal financial intermediation' function and its relationship to Jyothi and the moneylender is clear.

The 'do-it-yourself' nature of this device gives it its particular advantage over the other examples. There are no fees or interest payments. One gets back exactly what one puts in. Of course, there are other, non-monetary costs. Mary and her friends have to organize it, maintain trust and agree among themselves about the number of members and the size and frequency of the pay-ins, tasks that are not needed in the case of a commercial provider like Jyothi or the moneylender.

Mary takes her merry-go-round very seriously. The total value of the stock of her 'shop' is only a little over 1,500 shillings. Often, Mary has to dig into her working capital to pay for extra costs for her two children (Mary has no husband). But she can do so, safe in the knowledge that, provided she is faithful to her merry-go-round, she will get a 1,500 shilling lump sum within the next fortnight, and can then re-capitalize her shop. She once tried joining an 'NGO' that offered a bigger loan, but she found that its repayment schedule was too long to suit her needs, so she left. Instead, she joined another, longer-period ROSCA which she uses to build up her savings over a longer term, for use in schooling her boys.

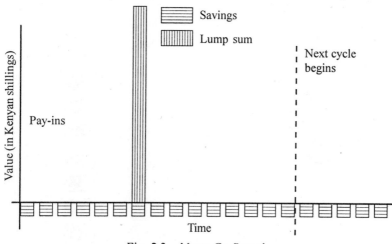

Fig. 2.3   *Merry-Go-Round*

Many ROSCA members in Nairobi join more than one ROSCA. This helps them get round a disadvantage of ROSCAs—an inflexibility in which everyone has to save the same amount in the same period, whereas individual households may have actual needs that vary in quantity and date.

SAVING UP AND DOWN: RABEYA'S 'FUND'

Is it possible to devise a type of 'basic personal financial intermediation' device that includes most of the advantages and eliminates most of the disadvantages of deposit collectors, moneylenders and ROSCAs? The last two examples in this chapter show two attempts to do so.

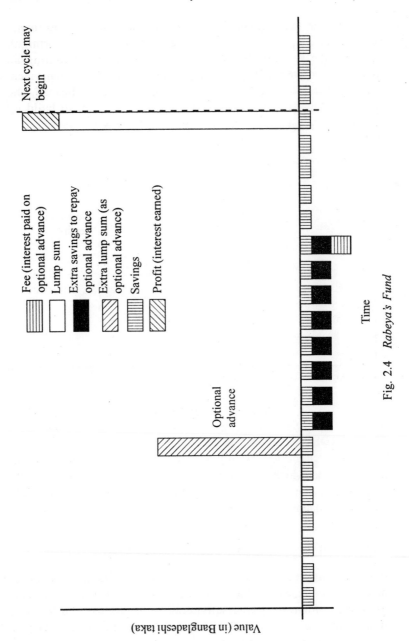

Fig. 2.4   *Rabeya's Fund*

We start with what the slum-dwellers of Dhaka, in Bangladesh, call a 'Fund'. This is a type of savings club that can be found all over the world. In many places, including Dhaka, it is the main alternative to the ROSCA among user-owned devices for basic personal financial intermediation. It differs from a ROSCA in that the savings that its members deposit accumulate in a 'Fund' from which members may borrow—but only if they wish to. Figure 2.4 illustrates such a Fund:

In Figure 2.4, both a 'savings-up' and a 'savings-down' element are visible. The series of regular pay-ins below the line result in the big pay-out at the end—a classic saving-up pattern. But you can also see an advance (above the line) against a series of additional pay-ins below the line, representing the savings-down device. Figure 2.4 is more complicated, and this reflects one of the disadvantages of Funds—they require more deliberate and careful management to make them work well. What follows is a brief description of how they work, based on what happened to a Fund that I tracked for some months in Dhaka in 1996:

In that Fund there were 23 members, all of who had committed themselves to save up on a weekly basis for one year, after which the Fund was to close. Each member chose how much to save, but it was always some multiple of 10 taka.[1] In practice, some saved 10, some 20 and a few were saving 50 taka a week (shown below the line in the diagram as 'weekly pay-ins'). As they came in, these savings were stored with Rabeya, the Fund's chairperson. Although a housewife, she had run many Funds in her neighbourhood, where she was well known. She kept a simple set of accounts in a school exercise book.

As soon as this cash in hand became big enough, members with a need or an opportunity for a lump sum were allowed to borrow from it (shown above the line in the diagram as 'optional advance'). The terms of these loans were straightforward—the borrower had to pay an interest of 5 per cent a month, and had to repay the loan before the end of the year (repayments and interest on loans are shown below the line in the diagram). According to the Fund's rules, decisions about who took this chance to 'save down', and how much they took, were made by the members collectively. In practice the Chairperson had by far the biggest say. She strove to make sure that everyone who wanted a loan got one, and that no member

---

[1] There are about 50 Bangladeshi taka to one US dollar.

borrowed an amount that was beyond, what she estimated he could repay (save down) in the time allowed.

At the end of the year, the total fund, including the interest earned on the loans made from it, was put on the table and shared by the members in proportion to the savings they had made. It worked out that for each 10 taka saved per week, members got back 580 taka (shown as 'pay-out and profit' in the diagram). Thus a member saving at the rate of 10 taka a week, saved 520 in the year (52 weeks) and got a 'profit' of 60 taka. Members got this profit on their savings irrespective of whether they took a loan.

How did this Fund perform in comparison with other devices? Compared to the moneylender the Fund's advances are—at 60 per cent APR,[2] instead of 180 per cent—a much cheaper way of borrowing lump sums. As a way of saving up, the Fund is not only cheaper than saving with Jyothi, it returns a good profit. One earns 11.5 per cent over and above what one puts in (instead of losing 9 per cent as with Jyothi).[3] This is an APR of plus 23 per cent (instead of minus 30 per cent with Jyothi).[4] As with Jyothi you can choose how much to save each week. But you do not get a daily visit, and you cannot choose your own start date, since that is a decision that has to be made collectively. Best of all, the Fund offers you *two* ways of swapping small pay-ins for lump sums, instead of one. You save up and withdraw, but if you wish you can save down by taking an advance as well. This double opportunity makes the Fund more

[2] 5 per cent a month is equivalent to 60 per cent a year. The formal equation for calculating APR is—professionals will note—different from the simplified (but useful) calculation I use. The law (in the UK) requires the use of the formula *(1 plus the interest rate for the period quoted) to the power of the number of such periods in a year, minus 1.* Under this formula 5 per cent a month is an APR of 79.5 per cent. $(1 + 0.04)^{12} - 1$), not 60 per cent. This allows for the fact that if you pay the interest each month and not in one lump at the end then you are out of pocket and the loan has effectively cost you more. This extra cost can be significant in loans on which interest is paid at short intervals, as in home mortgages in the rich world. My calculation ignores this sophistication, though where interest is paid at the end—as in the calculation in the previous footnote—there is no difference.

[3] If you are saving 10 taka a week you put in 520 taka in the year and earn an extra 60 rupees. 60 is 11.5 per cent of 520.

[4] If you are saving 10 taka a week then over the year you have an average of 260 taka on deposit. On this you earn 60 rupees. 60 is 23 per cent of 260.

flexible than the ROSCA—at the cost of more paperwork and management.

This added management burden makes Funds less transparent and more vulnerable to fraud than ROSCAs. Some conditions help to minimize this risk. For example, where Funds are very common the relationship between the amount users pay-in and the amount they receive at the end tends to become fixed. The ratios they use tend to converge so that almost every Fund in the area charges the same rate for loans and guarantees the same minimum return on savings. This 'institutionalization' of Funds makes it easier for poor illiterate people to know exactly what they're getting themselves in to.

Not all Funds are time-bound in the way that Rabeya's was. Some go on for an indefinite period. But being time-bound is a very healthy feature that good Funds share with ROSCAs. During a ROSCA or at the end of a time-bound Fund either one gets his money back or does not. If their ROSCAs or Funds do not produce the goods, the members walk away and the device dies. As a result, poor managers are soon out of a job, and members flock to others with a sound record. This makes sure that the majority of such savings clubs are reasonably well run, if not entirely without risk. I call this an 'action audit' and it substitutes very well for the sort of formal but less easily understandable audit that professional savings banks get accountants to do.

Funds can be wholly user-owned (run by the people that use them, as in Rabeya's case), or run by club officers on behalf of users, as when a church or social club runs them. They can also be run professionally, and some bigger church and trade-association Funds are more or less 'commercial' in that what they charge for the service generates a surplus, ensuring their continuity. We shall look at some examples in the fourth chapter. Meanwhile, our last example in this chapter is also a commercial one, and is a deliberate attempt to sum up many of the lessons of basic personal financial intermediation in one device.

SAVING UP AND DOWN, OVER SHORT AND LONG TERMS, WITH VARIABLE DEPOSITS: *Safe*SAVE

If we review the examples shown so far (Jyothi, the moneylender, the ROSCA and the Fund) in the light of what was said in the first

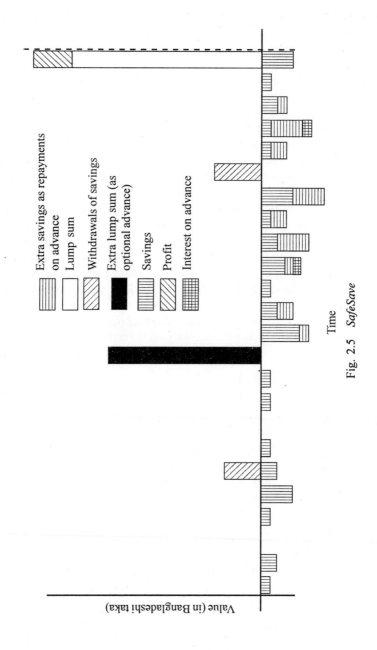

Fig. 2.5 *SafeSave*

chapter regarding the financial service needs of the poor, we shall find two ways in which the circumstances and needs of the poor are still not being met.

First, we noted that poor people need to store savings for the long run, for widowhood or old age or for their heirs. None of the examples shown so far helps them do this (or at least not directly).

Second, we noted that poor people's ability to save fluctuates with time, so that they may be able to save a lot at one time and very little at another. But in all our examples so far there is the requirement for a (more or less) *fixed* saving at a *fixed* interval (the same sum each day for each box on Jyothi's card or for Mary's ROSCA, or for each week for the moneylender or for Rabeya's Fund).

Both these shortcomings are difficult particularly for the *very* poor. It is the *very* poor who suffer most hardship in old age and need financial protection in the latter part of their lives. And many poor people get excluded from these devices—and often indeed *exclude themselves*—out of anxiety that they will not be able to save the same amount *every* day (or week, or month) for a *whole* year (or other period).

Figure 2.5 shows how *Safe*Save tries to get round these shortcomings.

*Safe*Save has Collectors (field staff) who visit each client every day at their home or workplace. They provide the same *opportunity* to save up that Jyothi and daily ROSCAs do and they also allow clients to save down, flexibly. On each occasion, clients may save, but in any amount they like, including zero. The 'pay-ins' in the diagram show this—they vary over time. From this accumulation of savings clients may *withdraw* a lump sum at any time they like—this is shown by the chequered black amounts. Then, as in a Fund, they can take optional 'saving down' advances. But—better than a Fund—clients repay when they like and can take as much time as they like—so long as they pay the interest each month. Finally, as in a Fund, they get a pay-out of their accumulated savings plus profits. But unlike a time-bound Fund like Rabeya's, they can leave these savings on deposit for any length of time and earn more profit the longer they leave them in. The only respect in which this flexibility is compromised is that they cannot withdraw from savings while they are holding an advance (except to repay the advance) and for this reason clients are allowed to hold more than one account.

The current version of *Safe*Save operational in the slums of Dhaka, Bangladesh, pays clients a little under 10 per cent a year on savings (much less than Rabeya's Fund but more than formal banks) and charges an APR of about 28 per cent on advances (much less than Rabeya's Fund but more than formal banks).

*Safe*Save raises many questions. One of them is whether *Safe*Save can be run profitably, generating surpluses that guarantee its sustainability and fuel its expansion. Unless this can be shown, *Safe*Save will not contribute much to banking with the poor. Though early signs are encouraging, *Safe*Save is still young—it began only in 1996—and more time is needed to see if it will pass this crucial test. No more will be said on this issue here, since this chapter is concerned with 'basic personal financial intermediation' and focuses on the user's perspective.

The main question raised by *Safe*Save in that context is *discipline.*

We have already seen that without discipline it is hard to save. This is true whether those savings are made 'down', following an advance against savings (as with moneylenders), or whether they are made 'up', and precede a withdrawal or advance (as with a deposit collector like Jyothi), or are made 'through'— both before and after a withdrawal/advance (as in a ROSCA). Moneylenders enforce discipline by their regular weekly visit, and Jyothi does it by daily appearances on the doorsteps of her clients. ROSCAs fail if their self-imposed discipline falters. *Safe*Save is no different, except that it has given up some things that undeniably promote discipline very strongly—*uniformity* of deposit size, and *regularity* of deposit. In all the other examples shown so far the user pays a set amount at a set interval. In *Safe*Save the user may pay at any interval and in any amount—including zero.

The risk is, therefore, that without any compulsion to pay a set sum at a set interval, *Safe*Save's clients will simply fail to save. *Safe*Save's experimental aspect is precisely that it is testing the extent to which a *frequent and reliable opportunity* to save is a way of maintaining savings *discipline.* So far, the indications are good. It looks as if the frequent opportunity to save—having someone knock on your door each day—is an equally good, or even better, way of maximizing savings, as compared to the obligation of paying a set sum at a set interval.

Box 2.4   Summing Up *Safe*Save

*Safe*Save is a deliberate attempt to set up a financial service scheme for the poor which meets their circumstances and needs as understood by this author over twenty years of research and practice.

It allows for the fact that the poor can save and want to save—but can save only in small (but variable sized) amounts and can't save each and every day.

It allows for the fact that the poor need to turn those savings into usefully large lump sums at both short and long-term notice, and sometimes without notice. It recognizes that to help them do this it must provide them—on a daily basis:

- the chance to save up (to save and withdraw)
- the chance to save down (to take an advance against future savings)
- the opportunity to store up savings for long-term needs

*Safe*Save recognizes that no one can save without discipline, and offers a daily opportunity to save to all its clients as a way of developing and maintaining that discipline.

*Safe*Save is thus the most flexible of all the examples dealt with in this chapter, and because of this, it is the most attractive to the very poor who can be frightened off by the need to pay set sums at set intervals.

It may occur to you that—with the exception of the doorstep service offered by its Collectors—the financial services *Safe*Save offers are rather like what is available over the counter to ordinary customers of banks in the rich world. It is a combination of current account, savings account, long-term deposit, and loans.

Should that surprise you?

CONCLUSION

This chapter has used actual examples to illustrate basic personal financial intermediation—the process through which people turn their savings into usefully large lump sums of money. Poor people need this process as much as anyone else, because poor people *can* save and poor people have frequent need, throughout their lives, of 'usefully large lump sums of money'. Other ways of getting hold of large sums of cash, such as being the beneficiary of charity, or selling or pawning assets, are either unreliable or unsustainable. The task of financial services for the poor, therefore, is to provide them mechanisms through which the swap from savings into lump sums can be made.

As an introduction to the wide variety of such mechanisms, the chapter has described three informal devices. Deposit collectors will accept people's savings and return a lump sum to them, moneylenders will provide the lump sum up front and then collect savings in repayment, and ROSCAs allow people get together to make savings from which each in turn takes their lump sum. Elements from these three systems can be combined to provide a more flexible service, as we saw in the example of Rabeya's Fund.

These devices are all time-bound, but poor people's needs for basic personal financial intermediation are never-ending, so many poor people are engaged, cycle after cycle, with their deposit collector, moneylender, ROSCA, or Fund. *Safe*Save, the last example in the chapter, illustrates one way of serving poor people's longer term needs for swaps, by allowing them to keep money on deposit for the long term. *Safe*Save, unlike the other devices discussed so far, allows savings deposits to be made as and when the saver has them in hand: the idea behind this flexibility is that the *very* poor, who may feel unable to save set sums at set intervals, can also avail of the service.

All the main ideas of my essay have now been expressed. If you wish to read on, you will find, in Chapters Three and Four, much more detailed descriptions of the kinds of devices that you can expect to find in slums and villages of the developing world. After that, in Chapter Five, I describe a little of the recent work that has been done by outsiders to bring more and better financial services to the poor. Chapter Six winds up the essay with some remarks on how to go about designing better financial services for the poor.

3

ROSCAs and ASCAs: Doing It Yourself

Savings clubs are groups of people who come together to set up and run their own basic personal financial intermediation services. There are two kinds of clubs—the ROSCA kind (where everyone puts in and takes out the same amount) and the 'accumulating' kind (where some borrow and others do not).

The world of money management for the poor is rich and complex. Schemes and services have long histories, and countless variations. Geographic areas have come up with solutions tailored to their particular social and economic conditions. As a result, it's not easy to categorize financial services for the poor. Nevertheless, this chapter and the next divide the services into three classes—*savings clubs, managers* and *informal providers*—a classification based on who owns and manages the services. The categories though not water-tight, are robust enough to be useful.

Savings clubs are composed of people who come together to pool their savings in various ways. These clubs are *owned and managed by their members*, and it is this characteristic that distinguishes savings clubs from the other two classes. There are, however, two main kinds of user-owned savings clubs. There is the ROSCA kind where the cash rotates evenly among all the group members (as in Mary's merry-go-round), as also an 'accumulating' type where some members borrow and others do not (as in Rabeya's Fund). For the accumulating (Fund) type I am going to use the name that Fritz Bouman gave them—the ASCA, for Accumulating Savings and Credit Association.[1]

Managers are those who run savings clubs for other people. Religious and welfare organizations often do this on a voluntary or non-profit basis, but there are also commercial managers, such as

---

[1] I used 'Funds' to describe Rabeya's savings club in Chapter Two because that's what their users call them.

those who earn a fee for managing ROSCAs for people—I call them 'chit managers', after the Indian name for the ROSCA.

Informal providers are a mixed bunch who have the common feature that they *provide* basic personal financial intermediation services to others. Deposit collectors (such as Jyothi), moneylenders (like Ramalu's) and pawnbrokers are examples. Usually they deal with users of their services on an individual basis, and most charge for their services.

Box 3.1 Classes of Basic Personal Financial Intermediation Services			
Savings Clubs (owner-managed)	*Managers*	*Providers*	
ROSCAs (where the cash rotates evenly between members)	ASCAs (where the cash withdrawal varies)	Includes religious and welfare organizations, and 'chit' managers	Includes deposit collectors, money lenders, and pawn-brokers

This chapter deals with ROSCAs and ASCAs, while the next describes Managers and Providers. A section on the ingenious 'ubbu-tungnguls' of northern Philippines, is included at the end of this chapter as a demonstration of the inventiveness of poor people when it comes to managing money—and as a reminder of how hard it can be to categorize their inventions.

The ROSCA

The ROSCA is the world's most efficient and cheapest financial intermediary device. The best form of ROSCA—the auction ROSCA—matches savers perfectly with borrowers, and rewards both of them.

With its description of Mary's savings club or 'merry-go-round', Chapter Two provided an example of how the poor can and do get together to manage their own basic personal financial intermediation. The merry-go-round is just one of the many variations of the ROSCA. ROSCAs are found in various forms on every continent, and have been in exsitence for many years. There are references to ROSCAs in Japan dating back six hundred years.[2]

---

[2] That is, before modern banking evolved in Europe.

This essay is not about the history of the ROSCA, nor does it offer evidence about the huge numbers of ROSCAs found round the world. As the bibliography shows, documentation is already available. Rather, having noted that the ROSCA is indeed an extremely popular intermediation device, this essay will try to honour it by describing as simply as possible its major variants and explaining their differences.

Anthropologist Shirley Ardener devised what has become the standard definition of a ROSCA:

An association formed upon a core of participants who make regular contributions to a fund which is given, in whole or in part, to each contributor in rotation.

Thus, in Mary's merry-go-round, there are fifteen members (the 'core of participants') each of whom make a daily contribution of 100 shillings. That daily total (1,500 shillings) is given in whole to each contributor in turn. The process takes fifteen days.

In what follows I use the word 'round' to refer to each distribution of the lump sum (the total number of which will equal the number of members). The word 'cycle' is used for the complete set of rounds, after which the ROSCA comes naturally to an end (though it may be repeated, with or without variations in the number of members, or in the amount and frequency of the contributions). In Mary's case there is a *round* each day for a fifteen-day *cycle*, and then they start another cycle.

The ROSCA's Advantages

The very elegance and neatness of the ROSCA gives it great appeal, and like many others I'm drawn to it partly for that reason. I joined a ROSCA in Mexico in 1974 and have been fascinated by them ever since. So they get first place in this chapter.

The virtues of ROSCAs are apparent in Mary's club, which neatly arranges the small daily savings of fifteen people into a series of fifteen large lump sums, which each member in turn enjoys. The ROSCA, which then ends (only to be reborn in another cycle), has no running costs and is wonderfully transparent—without elaborate books its accounts are clear to each and every member, even if they include the illiterate. No outsiders are involved, no one is beholden to anyone else, and no one has profited from anyone else's difficulties. Moreover, no money has to be stored by the managers of the ROSCA, because all cash passes directly from one member to another. This has two healthy results. Firstly, it greatly reduces the risk of misappropriation. Secondly, it makes ROSCAs extremely *efficient*. Indeed, ROSCAs can reasonably claim to be the most efficient intermediation device around, since at each round the savings of many are transformed instantaneously, with no middlemen, into a lump sum for one person.

Perceived Disadvantages

However, when people first hear about ROSCAs they often react by listing their disadvantages—as they see them. Usually, their first objection is 'what stops those who first get the lump sums from running away?'. The next is 'but the system is unfair—the ones who get the lump sum first have a huge advantage. They get an interest-free loan at their fellow-members' expense'.

We have already hinted at the answers to these two objections, in the first two chapters. People *like* to save regularly if they can, to build up lump sums, so even the 'end-takers' still benefit from a ROSCA compared to paying a deposit-collector like Jyothi or a moneylender. And people tend not to run away from services that they like. However, we shall be able to build even better answers to these objections by looking at the ROSCA in more detail.

Four Ways of Running ROSCAs

We start by listing the four main ways in which ROSCA users decide the order in which the lump sum is taken. They are by:

• prior agreement
• agreement at each round
• lottery
• bidding for the lump sum

Prior agreement: Mary's merry-go-round is a ROSCA by prior agreement. This type is particularly appropriate when the intention is to run many cycles of the ROSCA one after the other. After a few cycles, any 'unfairness' in the order has shrunk to insignificance, and every member's situation is the same—she gets her lump sum every fifteen days (for example). This pattern of prior-agreement multi-cycle ROSCAs is the dominant form of ROSCA in Nairobi's slums. It provides slum-dwellers with a secure way of saving *regularly and continuously.* Its simplicity—no decisions about the order of disbursement apart from the initial one need be taken, and no mechanism like lotteries or auctions are required—suits this continuous, routine savings function especially well. It means that members do not have to get together in a meeting each time the lump sum is taken, and many such ROSCAs run without meetings, or hold meetings only at the close of each cycle (which may also be the start of the next). This is indeed very convenient.

Agreement at each round: If members are well acquainted with one another ROSCAs may function as the type 'by agreement in each round', with a fresh decision about who gets the lump sum made at the time of each round, usually on the basis of who needs it the most. There are probably fewer of this kind of ROSCAs than any other kind, because of the difficulties of assessing 'need' without recourse to the price mechanism (see auction ROSCAs below), and the risk that the more articulate or the more cunning will manipulate the process.

But there is a variant of this type that is quite common, in which the ROSCA is initiated by someone who suddenly needs a lump sum and who gets friends to join in. Thus in the mountainous north of the Philippines I have met rural schoolteachers who go for many months without running a ROSCA, until one of them wants cash to furnish a new home and calls on her fellow teachers to start a ROSCA (usually funded from monthly salaries). She takes the first lump sum, and accepts responsibility for the management of subsequent rounds until the ROSCA finishes.[3] Some lottery and auction ROSCAs (see below) are also started in this way by an individual with a pressing need.

Lottery: 'Lottery' ROSCAs are a huge and varied class of ROSCA found almost everywhere. In some countries they dominate—Bangladesh is an example. The lottery avoids the problems of any perceived 'unfairness' in the order in which the lump sum is taken, or of comparing people's needs, by leaving that order to chance. Typically, names are drawn out of 'hats' (or the local equivalent).

---

[3] Such patterns of reciprocal obligation characterize many other cash exchanges that are not strictly speaking 'clubs'. Details of arrangements such as the *neota* of northern India, in which families are duty-bound to contribute cash for weddings among their neighbours, and then expect to receive the same help when they have a wedding, are reported in Jodhka (see bibliography) and are summarized in Rutherford [1996, 1]

Every member's name goes into the 'hat' in the first round, but winners are excluded from the lotteries of subsequent rounds. Obviously for the last round no lottery is needed, there being by then only one remaining member who hasn't yet received the lump sum.

The lottery itself also generates a certain amount of excitement, which brings a crowd of onlookers and in turn helps to make the process public and fair—though this 'festival air' tends to die down after a while. And of course members sometimes find ways round the arbitrariness of the lottery. Friends may agree to 'swap' (or share) their luck where one has a more pressing need than another, or one member may even 'buy' another member's lucky draw.

Precisely because lottery ROSCAs *do not* involve a group of friends deciding who among them most needs the cash, they can afford to have a more varied membership consisting of people who do not know each other very well, or who are complete strangers. In Bangladesh, a typical ROSCA in the capital, Dhaka, is run by a small-time shopkeeper who arranges the regular lottery. Not everyone comes to the meeting, and many members pay as and when they can, often between meetings, sometimes in instalments. The shopkeeper keeps the records of who has paid, and chases up late-payers. In the 'moral economy' of Dhaka it is not yet considered proper for such 'managers' to run ROSCAs commercially, so he (or she) bashfully accepts 'tips' from members as a reward for this work.

Bidding for the lump sum: By leaving the selection of 'winners' to chance, lottery ROSCAs are more flexible and less troublesome, and can cater to a wider variety of people and of needs than if the winner were to be decided round-by-round by group consensus. As we saw, however, members sometimes 'buy' a lucky draw from another member. But there is an even more flexible way to cater fairly to a wide range of people and their individual needs, and that is by setting up a market to decide who should take the lump sum at each round. This allocates cash to the member who most values it at the time, while compensating others by richly rewarding them for their patience. It thus benefits both those who are saving down ('borrowers') and those who are saving up ('savers'). It also elegantly arranges them in serial order with those who most need to borrow taking the lump sum at the beginning and those most content to save, taking it at the end.

This is how they work. Imagine a twelve-person ROSCA that meets monthly with each member contributing $10 (that is twelve 'rounds' for a twelve month 'cycle'). At each round $120 is available as the lump sum. At the first round those members in immediate need of cash choose to bid for the lump sum. Let us say that five members want the money, but the one who most wants it is willing to bid $24, and wins. She then takes $96 of the lump sum ($120 minus 24), while her bid of $24 is given back, in equal shares, to each of the twelve members,[4] who walk off with $2 each (thereby making a net contribution of only $8 that month).

As the rounds proceed, the size of the winning bid tends to diminish, since there are fewer people in the auction. This is so because, as in other ROSCAs, each member takes the lump sum—or a part of it—once only. At the last round there is no need of an auction, because there is only one member left. He gets the full $120.

The calculations for auction ROSCAs: Calculating how each member fares in such a ROSCA has caused arithmetic mayhem among the experts. I have made some simplifying assumptions and enclosed my calculations in a box. For those who don't want to be bothered with these calculations, the conclusion I reach is that both 'savers' and 'borrowers' do well. 'Borrowers' get their 'loan' at rates which compare well with those prevalent in the informal market, while 'savers' get well-rewarded, especially in comparison with a deposit-taking service like Jyothi's.

Figure 3.1 shows the first and last members in our example, at the same scale.

My suggestion that the auction is a way of ensuring that the lump sums go, in each round, to those who most need them sometimes provokes strong disagreement. 'Not so', say these critics, 'as in much of the real world, the sums go not to those who most *need* them but merely to those who can most easily *afford* them. In this way they merely perpetuate the conditions that the poor unfairly suffer in so many other aspects of life'. No matter how true that is as a general commentary on life, it isn't really true in the case of an auction ROSCA. After all, even the poorest member of all can still bid in the first round, and can win it if he is willing to accept the biggest discount. He is not disadvantaged by a richer member standing next to him with his pockets bulging with cash.

[4] In some auction ROSCAs only the eleven non-winners would share this discount.

Box 3.2   Calculations for an Auction ROSCA

Assume that the members who won the first four rounds each bid $24, members taking rounds five through eight each bid $12, and in the last four rounds there are no bids at all, so those members get the full $120. The bids total $144 (four times $24 plus four times $12). These bids are redistributed equally among the members, so each member gets $12 back ($144 divided by 12). The total amount contributed by each member must equal 12 rounds of $10 each, which comes to $120, less the $12 from their share of the bids, for a total of $108. *Contributions* are thus the same for each and every member. But the total amount *taken out* by each member varies. For example, the first member took out $96 on the first round, while the last member took out the full $120 but had to wait until the last round.

Now, examining the last member in more detail we see that he put in $108 over the year and then took out $120, so he earned $12 'interest' ($120 minus $108). He had on average $54 'on deposit' during that year. So he earned $12 on $54, that is a rate of just over 22 per cent a year. Not bad.

The first member also put in $108 over the year, but, as we saw, she took out $96 on the very first day. So she 'paid' $12 in 'interest' (matching what the last member 'earned'). Since she paid in an average of $9 a month she had 'repaid' her $96 'loan' in a little under eleven months. She thus paid $12 interest for a loan that averaged $48 over eleven months. This is an interest rate of 24 per cent over eleven months, or about 26 per cent a year.

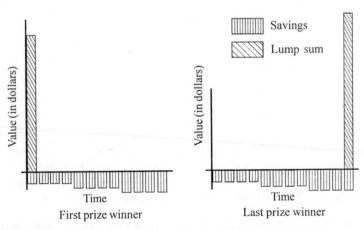

Fig.3.1   *Auction ROSCA*

The range of bid sizes in auction ROSCAs: The rates in the example above—26 per cent a year for a loan and 22 per cent a year on savings—would, in most countries, be more attractive than most other services available to poor savers and borrowers. But these rates are not *typical* for ROSCAs, they are merely examples to demonstrate the arithmetic involved. In practice ROSCA members often bid much *more* than the modest 20 per cent of the lump sum on offer used in the example above. In northern coastal Vietnam I talked to capital-hungry fishermen eager to invest in new equipment and found that in their ROSCAs, which are very common, early bids commonly reach 50 per cent of the lump sum, or more.[5] In other countries, notably India, bids are often so high that government has tried to limit them through legislation. Very high bidding means that net 'borrowers' pay a higher price for their 'loans' while those who choose to take their pay-out near the end receive very high implied rates of interest on their savings. ROSCAs are thus a very sensitive instrument for measuring, at frequent intervals, the price to the poor of capital in a local area (a point that economists and designers of financial services for the poor might note).

The ROSCA 'Sprint': Sukhwinder Arora noted that in the Indian towns that we were studying many slum dwellers were pushing money through ROSCAs (particularly auction ones) at a much faster rate than through any other type of savings club or financial service. He rightly describes ROSCAs as 'sprints', comparing them to more sedate services such as a savings bank, which he calls 'marathons'. In an ordinary savings account at a bank or Post Office you build up your savings gradually, over a long term, and it does not matter much if you do not save for several weeks or even months on end. In an auction ROSCA, by contrast, you commit yourself to the highest possible level and frequency of *regular* saving, by joining the ROSCA with the biggest contributions and most frequent rounds you can find (or that will let you in). For that reason the very poorest are the least well represented among users of auction ROSCAs. We noted in the previous chapter that one disadvantage of devices which require fixed contributions at fixed intervals is that the very poor may be scared off or prevented from

---

[5] Of course, members who bid high also, like the net savers, enjoy high returns on their deposits, thus offsetting their costs somewhat.

joining because of fear of not being able to maintain the strict schedule.

As you would expect, people with businesses favour auction ROSCAs as a way of getting hold of investment capital. People with regular incomes—above all salaries—favour them as a way of getting a good return on their regular savings. Businessmen can be fairly sure of being able to make the contributions at the fast pace required, and their businesses represent for them attractive opportunities for investment of the lump sum. In many societies running a business is seen as a male activity; hence auction ROSCAs are sometimes seen as 'men's ROSCAs', while lottery ROSCAs are for women. This is true, for example, in some South Asian cities. Salaried people may use an auction ROSCA as a place to store their savings on a month-to-month basis, and may chose to put the lump sum, when it arrives, into a permanent home such as a savings bank. In this way they can balance the advantages of high returns and some risk (the auction ROSCA) with high security but lower returns (the savings bank).

That completes our survey of the main ROSCA types. But there are some other characteristics of ROSCAs in general that need to be mentioned. They include questions of trust, innovation, and of the manner in which ROSCAs spread.

Trust, and the Composition of ROSCAs

Who trusts ROSCAs enough to join them? In Dhaka, as elsewhere, there are some single-sex ROSCAs, but most are of mixed sex. Some ROSCAs are run by very homogenous groups of people— workers on the same floor of a garments factory provide a good example—but they are more often composed of a mixed bunch of neighbours, family and friends. We will come back to this fact in Chapter Five when we consider Bangladesh's famous 'quasi-banks' many of which are groups that are very homogenous with regard to sex and class. ROSCAs, as they go on from cycle to cycle, tend to retain members who perform well, and shed ones that are difficult or slow in paying, while adding new members who are recommended by existing 'good' members. A rich mix of members of all ages and both sexes and of varying relationships results.

Where, then, does the 'trust' to run a ROSCA come from, if the members did not all know each other beforehand? It comes from *action.* Trust is not a commodity that can be imported automatically from some prior set of relationships. It is something that has to be built and rebuilt—and thereby reinforced—over and over again. People stay in ROSCAs because they observe, round by round, that everyone else is obeying the rules. Trust is more of a verb than a noun. Perfect strangers, coming together with the limited aim of running a ROSCA, can sometimes construct and practise trust more easily than people with histories of complex relationships with each other.

ROSCA Innovation

Of course, ROSCAs can and do develop safeguards against wilful cheating. In this respect, ROSCAs have proved very innovative. As far as we can tell, there were very few ROSCAs in Bangladesh until about 1980, but since then they have spread and multiplied very quickly. In so doing, they have spawned many new variations. 'Rickshaw ROSCAs' are a favourite of mine. Poor men driven from villages by poverty come to Dhaka where the only work they can get is to hire a rickshaw, for say 25 taka a day (about $0.63) and hope to earn a net daily profit of, say, 80 taka (about $2). In the 1980s such men—illiterate and new to the city, and without any help from NGOs or other sources—devised a standard ROSCA system which has worked to the advantage of many thousands of them. Groups of them get together and agree to contribute 25 taka a day to a kitty which is held, for the time being, by a trusted outsider (often the keeper of the stall where they take their tea at the day's end). Every ten days or so there is enough in the kitty to buy one new rickshaw, and that rickshaw is distributed by lottery to one of the members. The process continues until everyone has his own rickshaw. They have learnt how to adjust the number of members, the daily contribution, and the interval between rounds, to best suit their cash-flow and the price of a rickshaw.

But one of their finest innovations[6] is the rule that once a member has 'won' his rickshaw in a draw, he must from then on contribute *double* each day. There is a 'natural justice' in this, since now that he has his own rickshaw he does not have to pay to hire one, and he is therefore no worse off. It is seen as a fair way of

[6] Not practised by *all* rickshaw ROSCAs.

compensating late winners for their long wait. But the device has two other effects. It shortens the length of the ROSCA cycle. This is because by the time half the members have won their rickshaws, enough extra money is coming in each day to reduce by a third the amount of time needed between rounds. And it gives winners an incentive to pay up and finish the cycle quickly, so as to hasten the day when they can enjoy the full income from each day's work. Some hard-working single-minded men that I know came to Dhaka ten years ago as penniless immigrants, joined successive rickshaw ROSCAs and built up big fleets of rickshaws, then sold up and bought taxis.

How ROSCAs Spread—and Grow

One of the curious things about ROSCAs is the distribution and incidence of the different types. For example, take South Asia. In India, in the slums and suburbs of the city of Indore nearly all the ROSCAs Sukhwinder and I could find were of the lottery type. When we moved south and east to Vijayawada we found that most were auction ROSCAs. In some northern states of India the ROSCA in any form remains rare. In Bangladesh it seems the ROSCA was virtually unknown twenty years ago, and today, though there are tens of thousands of lottery ROSCAs, there are still no auction ones (as far as I know), and there are far fewer ROSCAs of any type in the countryside than in the towns. In some places the ROSCA, or one particular type of ROSCA, is identified with a particular social group—a profession, maybe, or an ethnic group. Finding out how these patterns have come about is a piece of research waiting to be done. So far, we have only guesses. There is a debate going on among archaeologists about exactly how agriculture spread from the fertile plains of West Asia to Europe. Did the idea spread from village to village, by copying, or did it require the migration of a particular 'farming people'?[7] Did the lottery ROSCA arrive in Bangladesh because Bangladeshis on trips to India copied what they saw others doing, or was it brought from India to Dhaka by one of the immigrant groups who have settled there?

---

[7] Genetic science is beginning to favour the latter explanation, whereas traditional archaeology has long accepted the former. Perhaps we should think of ROSCA types as 'memes'—the intellectual equivalent of the gene suggested by Richard Hawkins (*The Selfish Gene*).

However they spread, there is evidence from many parts of the world that ROSCAs are enjoying a period of spectacular growth. Inspite of the arrival of formal financial services, they are refusing to go away. Infact, they are increasing in both number and complexity.

The ASCA

ASCAs lack the clarity of ROSCAs, and so need more management skills if they are to run well. They may suffer more fraud. But their advantages are also significant: they offer the chance to use more than one type of 'swap'. Some are stable enough to arrange very long-term swaps lasting many years and this advantage means that they can be adapted to work as a form of long-term insurance more easily than ROSCAs.

Wonderful though they are, ROSCAs form only one of two large classes of savings clubs.

In a basic ROSCA, a number of people meet, each puts a sum of money on the table, and then all the money is given to one person. In the minds of the members is the certainty that this simple drama will be played again next week (or tomorrow or next month) but with the money going to a different member. In subsequent rounds the scene will be replayed until everyone has taken the lump sum once. And when there have been as many rounds as there are members, it is certain that the cycle will come to an end. ROSCAs are *symmetrical* and *time-bound*.

But what if you start with the same basic ingredients—a group of people coming together to put cash on the table—but leave out the symmetry that, in a ROSCA, compels you to hand over the cash immediately to one member? A Pandora's box of possibilities opens up. We could store the money, keeping it with the cashier or putting it in the bank. We could lend it to one of our members, or to more than one of them, or even to outsiders. If we lend it, we can, if we like, charge interest. But in that case how much interest should we charge? And how quickly should the borrower return the money? What will be the criteria for borrowing—can people take a loan for just anything, or are we all saving for a single purpose? Besides, is it even necessary to save the same amount each week? Why can't you and I save different amounts, or a different amount each week? Do we need to save any longer once we have built up a reasonable fund? And anyway, how long will this go on—for a year, three years, until we have enough for us all to buy a motorbike or until some contingency arises or for ever? And who will keep the accounts?

Put together any combination of this long list of variables and the chances are that somewhere in the world there is an ASCA that runs like that. Out of this infinite set of possible ASCA types, this chapter will describe only a handful. Interspersed among these descriptions will be a discussion of two of the biggest issues that confront any group of people who decide to set up an ASCA— *interest rates* and *longevity* (i.e. how long a life the ASCA should have).

Time-Bound ASCAs

We have seen an example of a time-bound ASCA when we looked at Rabeya's 'Fund' in Chapter Two. In this type of ASCA, members agree to a high level of standardization and discipline. Everybody saves on the same day each week, and everybody either saves ten taka or a multiple of ten taka. For accounting purposes, the Chairperson can think in terms of ten taka units, or 'shares', of which some members have only one while others have several: this is a useful device which simplifies the book-keeping task. The life of the ASCA is set, right at the beginning, at 52 weeks, and this is rigidly respected. Loans all carry the same interest rate, loans to outsiders are not permitted (since that is too risky) and all loans have to be 'in' by the end of the year. Despite a certain inflexibility that these rules introduce, in Dhaka ASCAs of this sort are beginning to displace ones with laxer rules. Why should this be?

In a time-bound ASCA there comes a time when the books must be closed and all the money finally and fully accounted for. This gives the ASCA some of the clarity and strength of the ROSCA, since the members either get their savings back (with profits) or they do not. ROSCAs have come to Dhaka quite recently, and are growing rapidly. Dhaka's ASCA-users have seen for themselves the advantages of ROSCA-type discipline. These days ASCAs that do not meet the ROSCA-like basic test—getting your money back—die quickly. An evolutionary shuffling process sets in whereby good Chairpersons (or committees) with sound books, like Rabeya, run ASCA after ASCA, and less skilled (or even fraudulently-inclined) managers do not get a second chance to muddle or cheat their members.

ASCAs That are Not Time-Bound

Muddling and cheating certainly goes on. There are some parts of the world—rural Bangladesh, for example—where better-off and more articulate villagers often cheat their poorer less-educated neighbours through the use of loosely organized and poorly run ASCAs. Taking advantage of the need of the poor to find a place to save, they pose as 'patrons', and collect savings over a period of time. But in some strange way those savings disappear, or for some unexpected 'reason' never seem to be available to the poor families that deposited them. Such unsatisfactory examples of ASCAs are rarely, if ever, time-bound: there is no specified moment when the members, without embarrassment, can get an 'action audit' and can make up their own minds about how well the ASCA is running. In villages of Bangladesh that I have studied (where the ROSCA is yet to penetrate the countryside), ASCAs of this sort spring up every now and again, fail, and then after an interval—so pressing is the need to save—another one starts up, only to suffer the same sad fate. It is partly for this reason that, as we shall see in Chapter Five, rural Bangladeshis so gladly accepted the much more reliable services offered to them by the Grameen Bank and its imitators.

But ASCAs that are not time-bound have their own virtues, the greatest of which is that they allow savings to be built up over the long term. Although ROSCAs (like Mary's) and time-bound ASCAs (like Rabeya's) can repeat themselves cycle after cycle, each cycle is complete in itself, and all the money has to be returned to the members. But as we saw in our analysis of financial services needs in the first chapter, poor people also need to save up over the long term for old age, for their heirs, for marriage, and so on.

ASCAs and Insurance

The poor also need to provide against emergencies, and ASCAs that are not time-bound can help with the task of insurance.

There are two ways in which financial services can offer protection against the risk of losses caused by accidents, ill health, emergencies, thefts and so on. One way is through savings and loans—that is, by providing a home for savings over the long term and by offering loans. In this case, people are helped to create a store of savings (on the one hand) and to secure rights to loans (on the other) both of which can be drawn on when needed. This approach deals with people on an individual basis, and provides a lump sum the size of which is proportional to the individual's capacity to save and or repay. The other way uses the device of *pooling*. In this case, deposits are taken from many people, but lump sums are returned only those who suffer a loss. The advantage of pooling, of course, is that the lump sums can be much bigger than what an individual could ever hope to save or repay in a lifetime, and are therefore more likely to be able to compensate clients for the whole of, rather than a part of, the loss they have suffered. Both systems can be described as 'insurance', but it is the second method—pooling the deposits of many to compensate the losses of a few—that characterises the modern formal insurance industry. Interestingly, informal devices rarely use this 'pooling' principle, and prefer the 'savings and loan' approach. Some authors—especially Jean-Philippe Platteau in a paper listed in the bibliography—argue that traditional communities dislike 'pooling' because they believe that all financial transactions should be based on 'balanced reciprocity'—the idea that individuals get back more or less what they are willing to put in. They believe that it is inherently wrong that some people should benefit disproportionately from the contributions of others.

Be that as it may, it is a fact that I do not have many examples of true 'pooling' among informal devices. I describe a formal insurance company that works with the poor using 'pooling' in Chapter Five, but among informal devices only the 'burial fund' described in the next chapter uses pooling. Among the owner-managed devices which are the subject of this chapter there are no examples of pooling.

We will continue to use the slums of Dhaka as examples, and look at the schemes that soften the losses caused to slum dwellers when their property is destroyed by fire (and in the face of other risks like having the authorities bulldoze your slum). Dhaka's slums are highly combustible. The houses and shops have woven bamboo walls, they sit cheek to jowl, and cooking is done inside, on open fires. It needs only a moment of inattention, or a naughty child, to set them ablaze. Once a fire has set in, it is likely to wipe out dozens of homes and shops at a time. Since there is no public compensation for residents and shopkeepers who lose out in such fires, some slums have instituted a form of self-help insurance that is, in essence, a type of ASCA.

In these ASCAs residents agree to save a set sum (or a multiple thereof) each week which is collected by a cashier and banked. In the event of a fire, the fund is withdrawn and distributed to members in proportion to their contribution. Figure 3.2 shows a fire insurance ASCA for an individual user.

Nothing could be simpler. The pay-out equals the total of the contributions paid in by the time of the fire. Bank interest is used to cover the expenses of running the scheme, so the user earns no interest. Because it is important to have immediate access to the cash after a fire, the fund is not lent back to members but kept intact and in hand in the bank. Run at this level of simplicity, insurance ASCAs have a reasonable chance of working well.

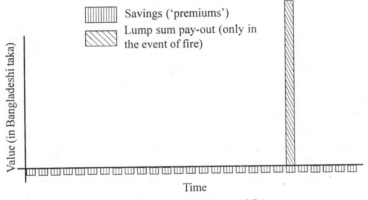

Fig. 3.2   *Fire Insurance ASCA*

The essential characteristic of an insurance ASCA is that the fund is released when—and only when—an identified contingency arises. This singularity of purpose is another aspect that adds discipline to ASCAs, and helps them to run better than more open-ended non-time-bound ASCAs.

Other well-running savings clubs also have single purposes, as we noticed when we looked at 'rickshaw ROSCAs' earlier in this chapter. Indeed, our distinction between ROSCAs and ASCAs begins to soften when we look at particular cases. Take the case of better-off slum dwellers who form savings clubs with the long-term aim of buying land on the outskirts of town and thereby escaping the slum. Regular pay-ins go into a fund that is put into a bank until there is enough to buy a parcel of land, and the process is repeated until there is enough land for everyone. Britain's 'Building Societies' probably had their origins in similar devices two hundred years ago. Members are not allowed to move onto the land—which is leased out meanwhile, often to local farmers—until the full amount of land has been bought, a device that helps to keep the group together for the long haul. This is very similar to the way a rickshaw ROSCA works, except the price of land changes over time. So members cannot be certain, at the outset, of how long their club will need to last, and the number and size of contributions cannot be fixed in the way that they are in a true ROSCA.

ASCAs and Their Interest Rates

Insurance ASCAs of the Dhaka fire insurance type are unusual among ASCAs in offering only one kind of swap—swapping savings for a pay-out. Most ASCAs offer two kinds of swaps, as we saw in Rabeya's case—saving up ahead of a pay-out, and borrowing ahead of repayment (saving down). This means they have to make decisions about interest rates, including both the rate paid to savers and the rate charged to borrowers. ROSCAs do not need to make such decisions, since they either ignore the issue (in merry-go-rounds and in lottery ROSCAs) or they allow prices to be set automatically by the bidding process (in auction ROSCAs). Before moving on to look at other ASCA types, it will be useful to discuss the issue of interest rates.

Well-meaning observers of savings clubs sometimes regard interest as, at best, a necessary evil. This is a mistake. Just as in ROSCAs the auction introduces a price mechanism that rewards savers and distributes cash to borrowers according to need, so in ASCAs interest rates can be used to manage rewards, prices and risk in ways that safeguard the interests of both savers and borrowers. The issue of interest rates is also important in determining the life-time of the ASCA, and whether it opts to be time-bound or not.

But just how are the rates to be set?

Well, Rabeya's ASCA charged 5 per cent a month for loans, which works out at an APR of 60 per cent. That may sound high to people living in rich industrialized countries where the hope is that such high rates are a thing of the ill-managed past (although rates not far short of this have been charged on credit-card debt, and are paid to loan-sharks by many low-income people).

Inflation makes it hard to compare interest rates across countries. ASCAs in high inflation countries have to charge more interest, to prevent their fund (and thus their members' savings) from suffering a decline in value. But we can observe that in countries with moderate inflation rates—as in the South Asian and South-East Asian countries over the last thirty years, for example—ASCAs typically charge in the range of 3 to 8 per cent a month, sometimes more. When I researched fifty of Dhaka's groups in early 1996, a time when Bangladesh's inflation rate was a modest 5 per cent a year, I found none that charged less than 3 per cent a month for loans. One charged an astonishing 20 per cent a month (admittedly, that one was not working well). But the single most common rate was 10 per cent a month—half the sample had chosen that rate. In the Bangladeshi countryside, however, where opportunities to invest money profitably are much less than in busy Dhaka, and where loans are taken for consumption more often than for production, rates are much lower, falling mostly in the 3–5 per cent a month bracket.

Interest rates on loans made by ASCAs affect the rate of growth and the absolute size of the club's funds. One does not always appreciate just how sensitive the size and growth of capital are to small-sounding changes in the interest rate. Consider an ASCA with twenty-five members who agree to save $1 a month each. Obviously after the first meeting they will have a fund of $25, and after a year $300 ($25 × 12 months). Now imagine that the ASCA decides to 'clear' all funds each month—to insist that it is *all* lent out to its members, so that no money is sitting idle, or in the bank. If they decide to charge members 1 per cent a month for these loans then their fund will have grown to $317[8] (rather than $300) by the end of the first year. By the end of the fifth year it will have grown to $2,042, and at the end of ten years it will stand at $5,751 (or $230 each, for a contribution of $120). Their money will almost have doubled.

---

[8] Assumes interest is paid monthly at the meetings and is immediately lent out. These figures are all somewhat simplified, and are therefore accurate approximations. Readers with a lot of patience and a good spreadsheet can recalculate the exact figures.

However, if this club decides to settle on an interest rate at the low end of the range commonly used by most poor-world ASCAs— 3 per cent a month—it could look forward to a much faster growth rate. But if it followed Dhaka's clubs and charged 10 per cent a month, the ASCA will own (in theory) a mind-bogglingly large fund after ten years. In the table below, which sets out these results, I have left one of the cells blank, to give you a chance to guess the answer before looking it up in the footnote.

Table 3.1

ASCA of 25 Members Saving $1 a Month Each and Keeping All Cash Out on Loan

Interest rate	Capital after 1 year (after contributing $300 in savings)	Capital after 5 years (after contributing $1,500 in savings)	Capital after 10 years (after contributing $3,000 in savings)
Zero	$300	$1,500	$3,000
1 % monthly	$317	$2,042	$5,751
3 % monthly	$355	$4,076	$28,092
10 % monthly	$535	$75,870	See footnote[9]

You will have noticed my cautious comment in parentheses—'in theory'—and it may already be obvious to you why I had to include it. However, real life calculations is quite different from arithmetical examples. In *reality* no club could sustain a policy of lending everything out to its members at 10 per cent a month for a period of ten years. It would mean that each and every member, at the start of the tenth year, would have to hold a loan of $325,000, and be paying interest each month of $32,500. That is obviously quite unrealistic.

What then would we realistically expect to happen, as time goes by, to ASCAs that start off charging high rates of interest on loans? Six likely paths are immediately apparent. First, they might reduce

[9] $23,177,017—each of the 25 members will have become almost a millionaire.

the interest rate on loans as time goes by. Second, they might decrease the amount they save each month, or stop saving altogether. Third, they might store their excess cash in a bank instead of lending it out among themselves. Fourth, they could risk lending their money to outsiders, given that their own members' appetite for loans at high prices would be quickly sated. Fifth, they might persevere with their high rate of interest, give out bigger and bigger loans, run into repayment problems, and collapse. Sixth, they might just stop, after a number of years, and share out the profits. Or, of course, they may take some combination of these paths.

These outcomes are indeed what we observe in reality. I have seen examples of all six. But experience appears to have taught many people that the last—winding the club up after some time—is the best. To see why, we need to look at the disadvantages of the other options.

If the club chooses the first option, and voluntarily lowers its interest rate, that can only mean that its members are less hungry for loans than they were, so an important function of the club has already been achieved, and enthusiasm for it will wane. The same can be said of the second option—lowering the rate of savings or stopping savings altogether. This option has another snag, because if the members are not saving regularly, the repetitive actions on which trust is built become less effective. The interest that can be earned in a bank is miserly compared to the rates the members have got used to earning on their savings through their loans to each other, so the third option is not very attractive either. Lending to outsiders at high rates of interest—the fourth option—is rarely sustainable in the long run because of the risk of loan loss, especially if the group doing it is composed of poor and not very powerful people. Collapse is to be avoided at all costs, since it jeopardizes each and every member's investment, so the fifth option is unthinkable.

So when the immediate appetite for loans is satisfied, and fewer members are willing to pay high rates of interest to borrow, many such clubs become 'time-bound' (even if they hadn't so intended at the start), wrap up and distribute profits after a few years.

Managing Risks and Rewards

These decisions can be seen as having to do with managing risks and rewards—balancing likely gain against likely failure. All lending involves risk. We have seen a few ways in which ROSCAs reduce the risk of members running off with the pay-out before they have paid their share of subscriptions. ASCAs are more complex than ROSCAs (on average). For that reason, they generally need more paperwork, and better monitoring of members. But also for that reason, there is a bigger range of ways in which risk can be managed.

In an ASCA, fresh money (as opposed to repayments of loans) comes in from two sources—the members' regular savings, and the interest they pay on any loans they take.[10] Setting interest rates adjusts the proportion of total funds that come in from these two sources. Low interest rates on loans will mean that most fresh money comes from savings, whereas high interest rates will tilt the balance so that a bigger—and· *growing*—proportion of fresh money is coming from interest paid on loans. Table 3.1 shows this quite clearly—at zero interest rates, all the fresh money comes from savings, whereas at 10 per cent a month current income from interest payments exceeds that from savings after little more than a year.

Thus where interest rates are high, a bigger and growing proportion of loans will be sourced from the interest payments of the borrowers themselves, and less and less from those who save but choose not to borrow. This means that if an ASCA is composed, as many are, of people who want to borrow and others who are content to save, adopting a high interest rate policy will ensure that the borrowers largely finance their own loans. In the event of something going wrong, savers may lose their hoped-for profits but they have less capital at risk. This can be useful sometimes, as the following story shows.

Initial-investment ASCAs: In the hills of northern Philippines, as elsewhere in the country, the government encouraged user-owned financial services in the form of village-level co-operatives. Unfortunately, these were not always well conceived or run[11], and have had the result of undermining faith in all savings-based devices. People became reluctant to trust their savings to ASCAs and other forms of savings club. But the user-owned tradition is hard to kill off, and another form of ASCA has evolved. In this, members make

---

[10] Some clubs also have entry fees, fines for late attendance, etc.

[11] Many co-operatives in The Philippines *do* run well. The country has been an innovator in credit co-operatives.

only one initial investment, which is often quite small. These investments are pooled and lent out at a *very* high rate of interest (up to 10 or even 15 per cent a month) to the member(s) most in need of cash. As those borrowers, and successive ones, repay their loans with interest, the fund grows quickly, and that growth is financed *entirely* from interest payments contributed by the borrowers. Those who contribute their initial investment but do not borrow can sit back and watch their investment grow—but they need to make their voices heard at club meetings to contain the risks of a high interest rate policy. In one ASCA that I looked at, they had done that by insisting that the club close down and distribute its profits after three years. Even after so short a time, at 15 per cent a month, a saver who put in only an initial $1 could see her share of the capital multiply 133 times. Figure 3.3 shows the cash flows for a net saver and the likely picture for a borrower in such a scheme.

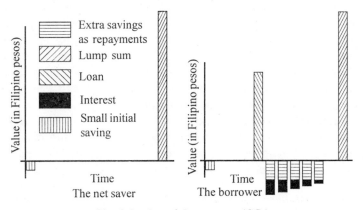

Fig. 3.3 *Initial Investment ASCA*

This example shows that the collapse of confidence in 'saving up' (saving ahead of a lump sum) meant merely that people stopped saving up—it does not mean that the *need* to save, which we saw in the first chapter is unavoidable for the poor—had gone away. If people were no longer able to find places to store and grow savings until they accumulated into a usefully large lump sum, then they had to find some other way of swapping savings for lump sums. (Some other way, as I would say, of getting access to basic personal financial intermediation). This other way turned out to be the initial-investment ASCA, a device that reduces the need to 'save up' to the barest minimum, but forces members to 'save down' at very high rates after getting hold of their lump sums.[12]

Reiteration, growth and permanence: ROSCAs and ASCAs offer hope and service to millions world-wide. But, we have discovered, not many of them are *permanent* institutions. All ROSCAs and, it turns out, many ASCAs, are time-bound, or end up with shorter lives than their members may have expected. Given that many modern writers on financial services for the poor are very concerned with the '*sustainability*' of financial institutions for the poor, it is worth pondering this fact. We shall do that now, before moving on to look at one form of ASCA that does aim at permanence—the Credit Union.

We could say that the 'strategy' favoured by user-owned clubs to reach out to millions of people (to adopt the intentionalist stance for time being) is 'reach lots of people through *multiplication*, and serve them continuously through *reiteration*'. Millions of individual clubs (ROSCAs and ASCAs) are constantly springing up, closing down, or reemerging. Formal institutions, such as Banks, are quite different: they aim to serve millions by adopting a strategy which might be described as 'reach lots of people through *growth* and serve them continuously through *permanence*'.

We shall return to this point in Chapter Five, when we look at the differences between the new wave of 'promoters' and 'providers'. But for now we shall raise the question, 'is it possible to have long-term or even permanent *user-owned* savings clubs?'.

The Credit Union—A permanent ASCA: Yes, it is possible, but it is not easy. And if you are poor, it is least easy of all, for reasons not so different from those indicated in the Chapter One explaining why poor people find it hard to save at home. As time goes on, and your collective fund builds up, all the difficulties that confront you in running an ASCA have the unfortunate habit of getting more acute. More and more accountancy skills are needed. As the stakes rise (with more money in the pot) the members are more likely to

---

[12] As it happens, northern Filipinos found another way of addressing the problem. This is the *ubbu-tungngul*—a device so intriguing that it is described in some length in the last section of this chapter.

quarrel over the rules and over book-keeping errors. As immediate borrowing needs are met, members are less likely to take all the available cash out on loan and more cash has to be stored. This is itself risky—if it is left with the cashier she might abuse it. If it is put in the bank that means more book-keeping, more work and lower interest earnings. As others in the slum or the village learn that your fund has now grown into a substantial sum it attracts more attention and thus becomes more vulnerable to theft or to more subtle attempts to get a share of it. No wonder a common response to these conditions is to say, 'OK, let us divide the money before things go wrong, and those of us who want to carry on can get together and start a new one'.

Yet there *are* examples of successful savings clubs that remain owned by their users, have a long life and become permanent institutions. They are all in one way or other members of a group of ASCAs known as 'Credit Unions' (CUs) or 'Savings and Credit Co-operatives' or 'Thrift and Loan Co-operatives'. To become permanent, such clubs need to be linked to a higher body that solves the set of problems set out in the previous paragraph. These higher bodies *supervise* and *regulate* the CUs, ensuring compliance with a clear set of rules. They offer CUs *financial services* that solve the problem of how and where to store surplus savings funds: this is often done in the context of an 'interlending' function that transfers cash from (usually older) cash-rich CUs to (usually younger) cash-needy ones. They may also offer insurance, especially insurance that relieves the heirs of members of any debt arising from a loan that is outstanding at death. Finally, they offer CUs *legal* registration, protection and representation and are able to lobby on their behalf with the authorities.

Because this set of tasks requires skills that demand education, fully-fledged systems of Credit Unions have rarely been owned exclusively by the poor. The poor have more often been members of CUs run by the educated middle classes. Fortunately, a number of CU higher bodies around the world are now taking a fresh look at how they can better serve poorer groups. My rather brief description of Credit Unions can be supplemented with the literature that these bodies produce (as listed in the bibliography).

With their several 'levels', formal registration with co-operative registries set up by governments, permanent salaried staffs administering interlending and insurance schemes, and links with formal banks, Credit Unions are clearly very different from the neighbourhood schemes like Rabeya's 'Fund'. In many ways they resemble the 'managers' that we're going to look at in the next chapter. In the last analysis, I believe they belong in this section, with the ASCAs, because, essentially, they remain user-owned savings clubs—entities that manage their own affairs as opposed to organizations that manage clubs for others.

The Ubbu-Tungngul

The chapter finishes with a curiosity[13]. As I warned earlier, some financial service devices are hard to classify. The ubbu-tungngul of northern Philippines is an example. Though it has many characteristics in common with the ROSCA it is not a true ROSCA because contributions vary across members and across time.

In the first chapter we mentioned that 'reciprocal' lending between neighbours is perhaps the most common form of informal financial transaction between poor people—I borrow a few cents from you today and on some other day you borrow a similar (but not necessarily identical) amount from me. If we wished we could do this on a regular basis: on the first day of each month I might borrow from you whatever loose cash you have, and on the fifteenth of each month you could borrow from me whatever I have available. But that does not sound very useful, does it?

Still, suppose I had a similar one-to-one relationship with many people, not just with you. I could agree with all of them that on the first day of the first month they will all lend me some cash—in different amounts depending on what they have on them. That would be useful, because the combined amount would be something substantial—it would be a 'usefully large lump sum'. Then I promise to pay them back, one by one, at fifteen day intervals. If there were ten of us then after five months I will have paid them all back and fifteen days later it will again be my turn to receive.

If you have followed my explanation so far, you will be able to see that each of the ten of us could in turn, every fifteen days, be the 'receiver' (of nine small varied amounts that add up to a large amount). On all other occasions each would be a 'repayer', giving a small amount to just one of the other nine.

---

[13] Since writing this book, I have been told that there is an almost similar device in Africa.

What would thus emerge, looks superficially like a ROSCA but is more flexible, in that it allows me to vary my payments according to what I have available in each 'round'. Of course, I have an incentive to put in as much as I can, so as to receive as much as I can when it is my turn. Keen ubbu-tungngulers might argue that this flexibility has the effect of raising the total amount transacted, since people do not have to limit themselves to putting in only what they are sure of being able to afford each and every round. The ubbu-tungngul shares this virtue with *Safe*Save.

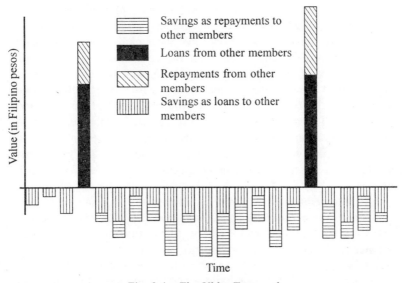

Fig. 3.4   *The Ubbu-Tungngul*

Figure 3.4 shows the ubbu-tungngul from the point of view of an individual member.

Each member is conducting a unique set of private deals with each of the other members, so why bother to go to the trouble of doing it in public at a regular meeting? Well, in part precisely because it *is* public and regular. Concluding deals in public provides a public record of the deal, which can be useful if a dispute occurs. Doing it regularly provides that *discipline* which, as we noted when discussing *Safe*Save, is very important to maximize savings, especially if the amounts saved are not fixed. The conclusion of several deals on the same day with a variety of partners also ensures something else—that the biggest possible 'usefully large sum' can be assembled at one time.

So we are back to where we started—financial services for the poor are ways of helping the poor to enjoy the *discipline* and *opportunity* to *maximize* their savings and turn them into usefully *large* lump sums.

CONCLUSION

This chapter has looked at how poor people form clubs designed specifically to meet their basic personal financial intermediation needs—their need to turn their meagre savings into usefully large lump sums of money. It is possible that these clubs, which are found on every continent and have been for centuries, constitute the biggest family of associations among the poor. I say this because I have been in many villages and slums where savings clubs have either been the only, or the most common, type of poor-owned association. The trust that is needed to run such clubs comes from each member's repeated (daily, weekly or monthly) opportunities to observe whether her fellow members are respecting the rules: this enables clubs to take in as members people who may not know each other well.

All these clubs use one basic ingredient—saving small sums over time—the basic ingredient of financial services for the poor. ROSCAs collect and redistribute these savings in a regular symmetrical way (the 'saving through' way), so that every member gets treated the same. ASCAs, the other large category of such clubs, are more flexible, and build a pool of savings which different members can use in different ways—to save up, to save down, or both. As a result of these differences, ROSCAs are better at assembling large sums quickly in the short term, while ASCAs are more easily adapted to serve longer-term ends such as insurance.

The more sophisticated versions of both ROSCAs and ASCAs use pricing methods that help manage risk and make the device more flexible and fair. The auction ROSCA elegantly and automatically allows the price to be set by the users each time a sum is distributed, and that price can vary over time. ASCAs have to deliberately 'set' their price, which they do by means of agreeing to an interest rate. In both cases, the best devices offer good terms to savers-down and reward savers-up well.

For good reasons, many savings clubs are time-bound. They still serve millions of poor people, by their strategy of 'multiplication and reiteration', a strategy that marks them off sharply from institutions like banks that aim at 'permanence and growth'. Nevertheless, if certain precautions can be taken, savings clubs can become permanent institutions, as successful Credit Unions have shown.

4

The Informal Sector: Managers and Providers

Some organizations manage savings clubs for other people. They often do it rather well, and are able to manage longer-term 'swaps' than simple user-owned clubs like ROSCAs and ASCAs. There are of course also many informal financial service providers, such as deposit collectors, pawnbrokers, and moneylenders, who deal with individual clients (on the whole) and usually charge for their services.

In the previous chapter we looked at that part of the informal sector in which groups of poor people organize financial services *for themselves*—by organizing savings clubs. This chapter is also about the informal sector and deals with those informal services that are used by the poor but run for them by others.

There are two kinds of people or organizations in the informal sector that run services *for* poor people. I call them the 'managers' and the 'providers'. The 'managers' include non-profit organizations such as churches, temples, youth or women's clubs, or trade associations, that are stable enough to run simple savings and loan clubs for their members. There is a category known as commercial 'manager' which runs ROSCAs for other people and takes a fee for doing so. The 'providers', by contrast, are people who offer unregistered financial services to the poor for sale: typically they are moneylenders or deposit collectors of the sort we looked at in Chapter Two. As usual, these definitions are not water-tight: as we shall see, some moneylenders lend more out of social obligation (or even as a way to save) than out of a desire to make profits. The chapter deals first with the 'managers' and then with the 'providers'.

THE MANAGERS

Permanent organizations whose main business does not involve providing financial services may nevertheless manage savings clubs on behalf of their members. Their status may allow them to do this rather well. Some commercial operators specialize in running ROSCAs for the general public.

I am using the term 'managers' to describe organizations that are not themselves savings clubs, but manage clubs for others. We start with welfare-oriented organizations that manage ASCAs, and end with commercial outfits that run ROSCAs. All the examples come from southern India.

Managed 'Funds'—The Annual Savings Clubs of Cochin

In the city of Cochin, in the southern Indian state of Kerala, you will find many slum-dwellers enrolled in clubs that closely resemble Rabeya's Fund ASCA. They save a set amount on a weekly basis (multiples of ten rupees) and do so for exactly a year. They may, if they wish, take a loan from the fund as it builds up, infact, many do so. These loans are priced at 4 per cent a month and must be repaid before the year end. We do not need to make a fresh diagram since it would look exactly the same as the one we drew for Rabeya in Chapter One.

The difference is that the Cochin's ASCAs (which are called, confusingly, Annual Savings Clubs, or ASCs) are not owned and run by their users in the way that Rabeya and her fellow members own and manage their Fund. Instead, they are owned and run by churches (incidentally, Kerala has a big Christian population), temples, mosques, and trades organizations, who establish and run them on behalf of their congregations and constituents.

Compared to Rabeya's members, people who use these ASCs have less control over them. They can not easily vary the interest rate, and they have little control over the membership. But there are important compensations for this. For one thing, the management tasks, including the vital tasks of keeping the accounts straight and chasing up non-payers, are done by others—parish or temple priests or welfare association members do it as part of their duties, though they are sometimes backed up by permanent paid staffs. For another, the process of 'institutionalization' that we noted at work in Dhaka

Dhaka reaches spectacular heights in Cochin. In every slum that Sukhwinder and I visited, the rates were the same. You got 600 rupees back for each ten-rupees-per-week saved, and loans cost 4 per cent a month.

Permanent welfare organizations that manage ASCAs for other people confer another advantage. We saw in the previous chapter that there are many good reasons for most true user-owned ASCAs and ROSCAs to have a short life. This makes it hard for their members to save up for long-term needs. When they do try to serve such needs they are often forced to offer a very simple service, as we saw in the case of the fire insurance ASCAs of Dhaka, which can not lend their funds out because they need it at hand in case there's a fire. 'Managers', on the other hand, as a result of their greater size and permanence, are much better placed to serve long-term needs.

Managing Long-Term Needs—The 'Marriage Fund'

I have in my collection a simple passbook printed in the rounded text of Malayalam, the language of Kerala. It is issued by a local fisherfolk's 'Development Welfare Co-operative Society' just outside Cochin, and is for their 'Sadhbhavana Marriage Aid Fund'. The first few pages set out the rules with admirable clarity.

The unmarried men, women and children of the fishing community can themselves join the scheme, or have relatives join in their name. In practice parents and grandparents commonly seek membership in the names of their infants. They choose a fixed regular payment—let us say the equivalent of $1 each week—and start saving. These savings build up and are released back to the saver when he or she marries, along with a dividend worth exactly the amount saved to date (providing that at least three years have gone by). In the meantime, if the savers need access to their savings for some reason, they can take and repay a loan from the fund that is building up.

Such schemes provide savers with a place to store savings over the long term, guarantee them a lump sum to be acquired at a time of undoubtedly great need and provide them a bonus too. Over and above this they offer their members the chance to take a loan when they need it. I have redrawn our diagram in Figure 4.1 to see how one saver might use such a club. I have assumed that he (or she)

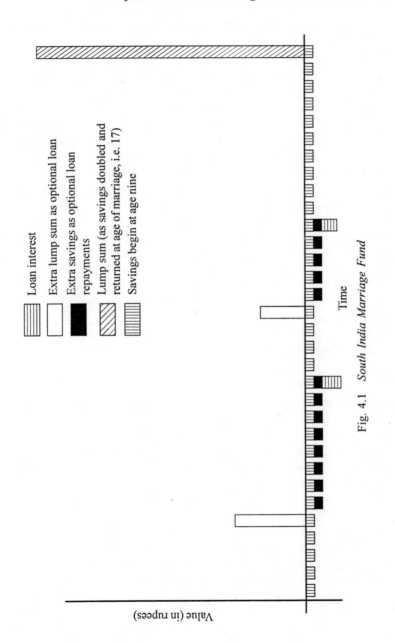

Legend:

- Loan interest
- Extra lump sum as optional loan
- Extra savings as optional loan repayments
- Lump sum (as savings doubled and returned at age of marriage, i.e. 17)
- Savings begin at age nine

Value (in rupees)

Time

Fig. 4.1 *South India Marriage Fund*

joined the club at the age of nine, married at 17, and took two loans during that time.

How can the Society be so generous? After all, if I join and save $100 and get married after three years, they will have to pay me $100 as a dividend. This amounts to an interest rate of 67 per cent a year.[1] But of course very few people marry three years after joining the club. Do the arithmetic again assuming that the *average* marriage takes place nine years after joining the scheme. The saver still gets double what he has put in, and of course he has put in much more, so the bonus is now a huge $300. The saver is happy— but the *rate* at which he has earned interest has come down to just over 22 per cent a year. That is less than 2 per cent a month. So if the Society lends out the savings funds at 4 per cent a month (as many do) it has a good 'margin' to cover its costs and any losses, even if it doesn't lend out its fund entirely all the time.

What about those who do not get married? Well, the Society has a rule that at 35 years of age you can take back your savings even if you remain single—provided you have been saving for three years. So if you started saving aged nine, by thirty-five you will get a big pay-out, no doubt, but the Society will have paid you interest at less than 8 per cent a year.

Managing Insurance Needs: Burial Funds

In a marriage fund, you save up for an event that is very likely to happen, and you do not get your money back until that event happens (or you get to be 35). In other words, the pay-out is contingent on a named event, and the fund is clearly offering a kind of insurance. Managed ASCAs can address these insurance needs more successfully than user-owned ones.

Alongwith its marriage funds the Cochin-based fisherfolk's co-operative societies offer 'burial funds'. These are even more obviously an insurance device. Some are time-bound and some are not. The working of the non time-bound version is similar to that of the marriage fund. It has a fund that grows over time and allows loan entitlements. The time-bound version, however, is different. It

[1] I have been saving weekly, so my average deposit over the three years is $50 (half the total I put in). On that $50 I am paid interest of $100, or 200 per cent. 200 per cent over three years is equivalent to 66.6 per cent over one year.

uses 'pooling', an idea discussed in the previous chapter. It is therefore a 'true' insurance scheme. It works like this:

As a member of an *annual* burial fund, I agree to pay a fixed sum each week for a year. If I—or anyone else in my family—dies during the year, the next-of-kin gets an immediate no-questions-asked pay-out, which is also a fixed amount. At the end of the year the books are closed. If the total weekly payments collected have exceeded the total pay-outs (which is normally the case) then the balance is re-distributed back to the members. If the total is less than the pay-out, members are asked to share the cost of making up the deficit.

When Sukhwinder and I investigated these burial funds, we found that the managers—often church or welfare society officers—made sure that each fund had at least 300 subscribers. With a smaller number, the fund was prone to run out of cash if there was an above-average number of deaths in the first few weeks. Given that one subscription covered everyone in the family (the member, his wife/husband, father, mother, unmarried children, unmarried brother and sister, other dependants, etc., as specified in the Sadhbhavana rules) we were puzzled as to how the clubs could calculate the likely number of deaths (the 'actuarial' analysis). The answer was, by experience. Many churches, clubs, temples, mosques, and trade associations have run such funds over many years, and the ratios have been learnt over time. The ratio is 1:500—for every 1 rupee contributed per week there would be a pay-out of Rs 500 per death.[2] This ratio cropped up over and over again as we went round asking about different funds—another example of what I have called 'institutionalization'.

As we have seen, the total contributions were normally found to have exceeded the total pay-outs, and this was intentional. For the managers, it is easier to give back excess cash than collect a

---

[2] The parents of babies who die within three months of birth do not benefit, and the pay-out for minors over three months is half that of adults. Paying fifteen rupees per thousand per year for life assurance (this was our calculation of the effective cost of such schemes for a six-person household) is expensive relative to the big government-run insurance companies (life assurance remains a public monopoly in India). But the government companies do not turn up at the bereaved household on the very day of the death bearing the cash, a bunch of flowers, and neighbourhood sympathy.

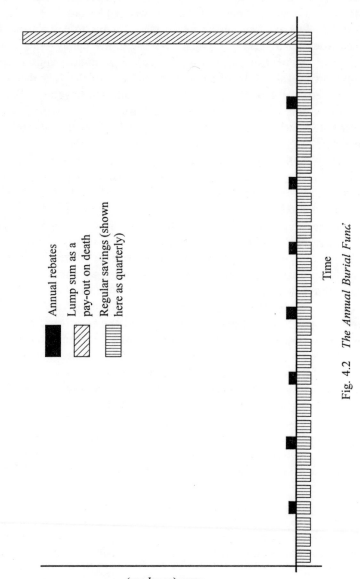

Fig. 4.2   *The Annual Burial Fund*

shortfall. And giving back cash has another healthy effect: it gives the members the impression that the club was run well, and provides with a little cash to make their first subscription for the following year.

At that time in Cochin, the minimum weekly pay-in for a burial fund was Rs 2, or about 4 cents US. If that was too little for you, you simply took out two or three or more memberships (or shares). Because the minimum was set so low, we found that these burial funds reached a poorer group of clients than any other savings club or financial service provider in Cochin. In some slums it was hard to find people who were not members of a burial fund. Fear of imposing a financial burden on the family at the time of death is very common among the elderly poor—especially widows—all over the world,[3] and this simple device much assuages that anxiety.

Figure 4.2 is our usual diagram, adjusted to describe the time-bound burial club. We have shown eight years, with a death occurring during the eighth year. As in the previous diagram, for presentation simplicity the weekly payments have been shown in quarterly summaries.

Managed ROSCAs

Mary (in Chapter Two) ran her own merry-go-round with fourteen friends. But we noticed that in Dhaka most ROSCAs have an informal manager of some sort, and this is the more normal case. It is not a very long step from informal managers having specialists who run ROSCAs for other people on a professional fee-paid basis. It has not happened in Bangladesh yet (as far as I know) but it is very well established indeed in India, especially in the southern parts. Sometimes a slum-dweller or a middle class resident will run these 'chits' (as they are known) for their neighbours on an informal but profit-seeking basis. However pawnbroking goldsmiths and, above all, specialist 'Chit Houses' run them under licence from the State government.

They initiate the chit (the ROSCA) and take the responsibility to find the members—who may not and probably don't know each other. They then ensure that the contributions are made on time. These are all auction chits, so the company also arranges the auction at its offices. They earn a fee from the auction winners when they take their lump sums. The chit company itself doesn't

---

[3] That is, not just in Hindu societies.

put up any capital—its contribution is in the form of the management skills and the willingness to take a risk, since some members may try to evade the responsibility to pay back.

In the big cities, like Chennai or Hyderabad, where there are thousands of chit houses, the poor and the very poor are not the principal customers. These chits are usually 'bigger' than they can afford—with monthly contributions of thousands of rupees. But many middle-class Indians use commercial chits to buy a lump sum quickly, perhaps to part-finance the purchase of house or a marriage. They find this easier than going to a bank. There is also a class of professional chit 'investor'—people who 'play' the chits to extract the biggest income from them. They do this by judging the best time to bid. The 'best time' will be a trade off between leaving their cash in the kitty as long as possible in order to gain the biggest discounts for the smallest bids, and taking it out quickly so as to move their money into a more profitable home. In this way chits compete with other forms of investment such as the Mumbai stock exchange, and I have been told by chit managers that the amount of money flowing into chits can be correlated with the fluctuations of Mumbai's exchange index.

THE PROVIDERS

Some informal financial service 'providers' offer deposit-taking: many others offer a bewildering variety of loans. All allow the poor to build usefully large lump sums out of their savings. Most providers prefer to deal with individuals, and most charge for their services, even though they are not always driven by the profit motive. In general, urban services are more professional, more precise and more disciplined than the rural counterparts.

There are many ways of provisioning informal financial service, and this section doesn't aim to list them all. Instead, I have classified them into four categories, and in discussing them I shall try to illustrate the particular version of basic personal financial intermediation that each of them provides. The first category is deposit collection (for 'saving up', like Jyothi's work in Chapter Two). The other three are all advances (saving down) of one sort or another. The second category offers advances against savings, like the urban moneylender described in the second chapter. The third and fourth offer advances against assets—existing assets in the case of pawn and mortgage (category three), and future assets in the case of crop advances (category four). The is summed up in Table 4.1.

Table 4.1
Four Types of Informal Provision of Financial Services

1.	Deposits	Deposit collection (saving up) *the collection and storage of savings deposits.*
	Advances	(saving down)
2.		Advances against a flow of cash deposits *a lump sum given in return for a series of small sums.*
3.		Advances against assets *pawnbroking and mortgaging.*
4.		Advance sale of produce *a lump sum repaid from the crop harvest.*

Note that these are types of provision, not types of providers. Many providers offer more than one service.

Deposit Collectors

Jyothi's service, described in Chapter Two, illustrates the basic need for deposit collection and how that need can be met by an informal provider. We do not need to add much here. Such services are widespread, though not universal. Although our example came from India, deposit collectors appear to be much more common in Africa, especially West Africa, than in Asia, for reasons that are not well understood. Perhaps they are still on their way, and most Asians will have to wait for a few more years.

In West Africa deposit collectors are found in rural as well as urban settings, and their recent growth in Nigeria demonstrates how seriously they are taken as a direct competitor to formal savings banks. There, male bicycle-mounted daily deposit collectors known as *alajos*, have seen their business grow as more and more formal banks have got into trouble. Like Jyothi, the *alajo* uses the discipline of a set saving sum, normally in the range of 50 to 75 cents per day. His way of collecting his fee is also designed to encourage his clients to save regularly, since he charges one day's deposit per month, irrespective of how many times the client deposits. Thus for the clients the more they deposit the lower the fee as a proportion of the cash handled. But unlike Jyothi, he allows his clients to withdraw whenever they like. In this respect his service is more flexible, more like *Safe*Save's. *Alajo* clients are well served: they are given a daily inducement to save, backed by a daily opportunity to withdraw. This is basic personal financial inter- mediation in a very pure form. Clients seem to like it: asked about the inherent risk of using a dishonest *alajo*, they are reported to have remarked that many banks—whose services are in some way inferior to the *alajo's*—are dishonest, too.

Advances against a flow of deposits: Some *alajos* store the cash they collect in (reliable) banks, while others offer cash advances to their clients. In this latter service they resemble the urban money- lender described in Chapter Two and, the two together illustrate our second category of informal provider.

   The urban moneylender has his rural equivalent, though in many countries there are interesting differences, in both the services offered and the providers themselves. Here, we will look at two of these differences.

   Urban moneylenders are more likely to insist on a regular periodic flow of repayments (though by no means all do so), as in the case of Ramalu's moneylender illustrated in Chapter Two. This may be because city incomes, even for the very poor, are often small but frequent, so that clients are more able to repay advances both from savings out of income in-flows, and savings out of regular expenditure outflows. The moneylender can tap the rickshaw driver's daily income as well as his wife's housekeeping. In the countryside this is seldom the case, because incomes for small farmers are more 'lumpy' (are received in bigger sums at less frequent intervals). Rural moneylenders are therefore more willing to let borrowers repay irregularly and infrequently.

   They are able to do this because clients in many rural areas remain less anonymous than the cities. The moneylender in the village is more likely to know intimately the borrower and his family. As a result, he has less need for the discipline of regular instalments to ensure the repayment of advance.

This leads us to the second common difference between the urban and the rural scene. Though there are many casual loans given and taken in the slums, the urban moneylender is more likely to be a *professional* than his rural counterpart, deriving a part if not all of his income from his moneylending services. The rural equivalent is much more likely to be a part-timer. Rural moneylenders tend to be formal salary-earners (both active and retired-with-a-pension), traders, and middle or larger-scale farmers. Few earn the majority of their income from moneylending. Many would rather not lend money at all, but do so out of a sense of obligation. It is very hard for a moderately well-to-do villager to refuse a loan to a very poor relative or neighbour whose child has fallen ill or who has nothing to eat in the house. This does not mean that there are no rapacious rural moneylenders—there are, and there is a reference to some literature on such people in the bibliography.

Yet another reason for lending money in the countryside is to *store* it. If you have excess cash and no safe place to store it at home, then why not lend it to a trusted family member or neighbour who needs it?[4] We saw in our description of 'saving down' in Chapter One, that many 'loans' are, from the borrower's point of view, simply an inverted way of saving. We now see that loans, from the lender's point of view, can be just a way of saving.

The combination of reasons for rural moneylending—out of *obligation*, as a way of *saving* and out of a desire to *profit*—make up a rich but hard-to-define picture of rural moneylending which varies from country to country.

A typical rural situation is illustrated by a moneylending couple whom I have been visiting regularly in northern Vietnam for five years. An educated couple, shrewder and more ambitious than most of their neighbours, they own and run a shop in a small village in a

---

[4] Imran Matin has pointed out to me, on the basis of his work in rural Bangladesh, that many informal rural lenders do not like to take their loans back in small instalments, because they think they will waste them on trivial expenditure. Like their clients, they too prefer 'usefully large lump sums'.

remote mountainous area. Their shop has been expanding gradually and they have added other small enterprises to it. They have always lent out money, but as their own fortunes have fluctuated, they have done so with more or less enthusiasm. Twice they have told me that moneylending is a fool's game, too risky to be worth while, and that they are about to give it up. At other times they told me that their loans are doing well. They prefer to lend modest sums (not more than $300) to other prosperous villagers engaged in developing assets like fish ponds or orchards. They also lend much smaller sums, reluctantly, to the poor. In each case they lend only to those well known to them. They charge 6 per cent a month, but claim to have incurred losses on loans to both kinds of borrower. They do not have set repayment intervals, and are obliged to chase borrowers and take whatever repayments are made at whatever time. Their transactions are part of the rural conventions. Whereas professional urban moneylenders offer an unambiguous financial service, in most cases rural moneylending is a 'service' only in the extended sense in which we can say that petty borrowing and lending among family and neighbours constitutes a 'service'. Rural moneylending can be basic personal financial intermediation at its most diffuse.

Advances against assets: The most common forms of advance against an asset are pawnbroking in the towns and land mortgage in the countryside—though of course just about any asset can be pledged as security for a loan.

Urban pawnbrokers prefer to lend against precious metals. A typical pawnbroker in non-Muslim South Asia, for example, will work from the shop of a goldsmith or silversmith and will lend against gold, silver and brass. As a smith he will have the skill and the chemicals to test the metals for their value. He will have a different interest rate for each metal. A customer taking a gold ornament to the pawnbroker will expect to receive around two-thirds the market value of the gold, and for each month he holds the loan he can expect to pay 3 per cent of the loaned amount in interest. For a loan against a silver 'pledge' he might pay 5 per cent a month, and 9 per cent for one against brass. In India brass is a popular metal for cooking pots, so many poorer families can get a quick loan against their kitchen utensils. Perhaps for this reason some pawnbrokers now take aluminium pledges: aluminium is rapidly replacing brass as the favourite metal for cooking pots.

Speed is an important characteristic of urban pawning. Unlike advance money against a flow of savings, an advance against a physical object does not require the prior knowledge of the customer, so the deal can be struck on the spot with a stranger (though the sensible pawnbroker needs to feel confident that he is not accepting stolen goods). This anonymity is another advantage of pawning, from the customer's point of view, since the neighbours don't need to know the reason for the pawn, which might be embarrassing.

Speed and anonymity are enough to ensure that pawnbroking will remain popular, even in those countries where governments have driven it underground by banning it.[5] But as a basic personal financial intermediation service it has snags, too. As we remarked in the first chapter, pawning is of use only to those who have something to pawn, so the size of the transaction is limited by the value of assets the customer already holds. Moreover, unless you have a particularly friendly pawnbroker, you have to take the whole of the loaned amount back to him to get your asset back, so to amass that sum you may need *another* basic personal financial intermediation device, such as a deposit collector or moneylender who helps build that sum from your flow of savings. If you can not do this, you run the risk of losing the asset entirely.

When the pawnbroker takes the pledged gold ornament from his customer he does not *use* it: he *possesses* and stores it until the customer reclaims it or it is clear that the customer is not going to reclaim it. In that event the pawnbroker sells it or melts it down and uses it as raw material in his smithy. In the countryside, when land or assets are given as security ('mortgage') for a loan, there are various combinations of use and possession. Sometimes merely an 'interest' in land is 'conveyed' to the mortgagee (the creditor), while the mortgagor (the landowner who becomes the debtor) continues to use it, just as a house-buyer in the west lives in the house he has mortgaged to the company that gave him a loan to buy the house. More commonly, the mortgagee takes over and uses the land, though he might choose instead to claim a share of its

---

[5] Some governments have lifted the ban. The Sri Lankan government, noting the success of private pawnbroking, has itself gone into the business, and set up shops around the country. It is said that this has increased competition and brought down the cost of the service.

produce. If the asset is not land but—for example—a tree, or even a cow, the fruits of the tree or the young or milk of the cow may belong to the mortgagee for the duration of the deal. The variations are endless.

From the point of view of poor mortgagors, land mortgage suffers from similar drawbacks as pawning—it is limited by the value of the assets already in their possession, and carries the risk of losing them forever. It is difficult to amass the sum of money required to redeem the asset, and simple devices to help the poor do this (such as those provided by deposit collectors or cash moneylenders) are in short supply in the villages, as we have seen. Then again, because of the legal procedures involved the deal can take a long time to conclude, and the illiterate poor are put at a particular disadvantage and can be cheated. As with advances against savings, conditions for advances against assets are generally less accessible to the rural than to the urban poor, and the devices available are less precise, less quick, and less reliable.

Nevertheless, asset mortgage is commonly practised in many villages world-wide, suggesting that the supply of more convenient financial services remains inadequate. Despite this, it is not always the case that the poor are mortgagors dealing with exploitative wealthy mortgagees, as the example of the *kat* deal in Bangladesh reveals. A *kat* is an open-ended land mortgage in which the mortgagee, in return for a lump sum, enjoys the use of the land until the mortgagor returns the sum in full. It is often used by middle-income rural families to get out of farming and into some off-farm business—perhaps a small shop in the nearby town or in the capital. They raise capital by concluding *kat* agreements with a number of poorer families amongst whom they parcel out their land. A poor family who can raise a bit of capital—often through joining one of the new wave of rural providers that we shall examine in the next chapter—can use the deal to get access to land on the long term.

Advance sale of produce: A poor farming family needing cash to get them through the growing season can, in many countries, raise money against the expected harvest. For many such families, this is the most common kind of financial transaction. It is often common enough for regions to have a special name and standardized prices. In some parts of Indonesia, for example, it is called *ijon*. In southern Bangladesh I observed that for many years in the 1980s the standard practice was for the lender to take one *mon* of paddy (about a hundredweight) for each 100 taka borrowed. Given a growing season of five months and a post-harvest market value for paddy of about 200 taka per *mon*, this represents an interest rate in the order of 20 per cent a month.

In such deals it is not as if the loan is given specifically for crop input costs. The family that takes the loan *might* use it to purchase seeds, pesticides and fertilizers, but they are just as likely to use it to feed themselves while the crop is in the ground, having exhausted their reserves in investments during the planting season. They might also use it in some other way, such as financing of life-cycle needs like marriages and others, that we listed in the first chapter. In terms of basic personal financial intermediation these arrangements represent an extreme case. The lump sum is taken for any of the normal needs, but is matched not by a *flow* of repayments made out of savings, but by one single large act of saving made out of the family's largest single lump of income—the harvest.

The provider of the advance might be any one of the set of moneyed villagers that we listed when we looked at rural money-lenders—salaried people, pensioners, big farmers, traders, and so on. But he might well be a paddy trader, and use the advance to further his business. Such arrangements can lead to long strings of lenders-and-borrowers. I looked at this phenomenon when I investigated the *dadon* system in southern Bangladesh, through which prawn production is financed. There, a poor villager with a prawn pond may accept an advance against his future production of prawns from a small prawn trader. The trader thus extracts a promise from the borrower that he will sell all his prawns at an agreed price to the lender. That small trader may himself be indebted with similar conditions to a bigger trader in the nearby town who may be indebted to a major wholesaler at the export port where the freezing plants are located, and he in turn may be in debt and so on up to wealthy absentee financiers with mansions in the more expensive parts of the capital.

Such systems illustrate the complexity of informal finance, and hint at its importance in national economic life. They take us away from basic personal financial intermediation, however, and will not be pursued further in this essay.

CONCLUSION

This chapter and the previous one have demonstrated the wide variety of ways in which the basic financial intermediation needs of poor people, who do not have access to formal services, have been met within the informal (including the 'do-it-yourself') sector.

But apart from satisfying our curiosity, how does this knowledge help us in the task of setting up more and better financial services for the poor.

It does so in three main ways:

First, it shows how patchy the distribution of available services is within the informal sector. Some slum dwellers and villagers enjoy services that are quite unavailable to their counterparts in neighbouring countries, or even within the same country or district. Geographically, then, financial services for the poor still have a lot of territory to cover.

Second, it shows the extent to which informal services have been able to react to specific differentiated financial service needs. But these too are unevenly distributed: in any one city or village some poor people will have access to deposit services, others to basic loan services, others to insurance services, others to several different kinds of services at once—and some to no services whatsoever. In terms of product variety, then, financial services for the poor still have a long way to go.

Thirdly, it shows that the informal sector has already reached levels of sophistication in handling technical issues such as the setting of interest rates. In many cases, this level of sophistication is well beyond anything achieved so far by the recent wave of new organizations aiming to provide services to the poor. Those new organizations are themselves the subject of the next chapter.

5

Promoters and Providers: New Ways to Manage Money

There is now a large and growing number of organizations interested in selling banking services to poor people, or helping poor people to set up their own services. These constitute the 'semi-formal sector'. Village Banks also fall in this category.

The first two chapters showed that the poor need financial services, especially of the basic sort that helps them swap their savings for lump sums of cash. Some poor people already enjoy access to such services, and the third and fourth chapters showed us how they do so—mainly by running their own savings clubs of one sort or another, or by using informal managers and providers. Such systems have a long history, but they are still very much in use and many appear to be growing in number, spreading from place to place, and evolving vigorously.

Savings clubs and informal managers and providers dominate the market in financial services for the poor. Formal banks or other formal institutions have, until recently, largely ignored the poor. However, the poor have never been left *entirely* to their own devices. There has always been public concern at the antics of cruel moneylenders (think of Shylock in Shakespeare's play *The Merchant of Venice*). There has also been a long history of official concern about poor debtors. Britain's colonial administrators regularly fretted about them and in many colonies introduced legislation against 'usury' (exploitative moneylending). There was a partial shift from a 'moral' to a 'development' motivation after the second World War, when many governments and donors devised rural credit schemes designed not only to protect the poor from moneylenders, but to assist them in adopting new farming techniques. Much of this effort had disappointing results.

But from the 1970s onwards newer forms of 'pro-poor banking' have been devised. By the mid-1990s there were enough of them, and they were receiving enough attention from aid agencies and governments, to hold an expensive international meeting in Washington, D.C.[1] to publicize their work, attract more support, share ideas, and set targets. Together, they constitute the 'semi-formal' sector. Some are beginning to call themselves 'microfinance institutions' (MFIs): others remain NGOs or government agencies.

This chapter is about their work. It begins by placing them on a continuum with *promoters* at one end and *providers* at the other. 'Promoters' are those who help the poor set up their own poor-owned or poor-managed systems, while 'providers' are those who *sell* financial services to the poor. The chapter is divided into two parts each focussing on one of these two ends of the continuum. In the course of the chapter comes a discussion of a type—the 'Village Bank'—that falls mid-way along the continuum.

THE PROMOTERS

Why not help poor people who don't yet run ROSCAs or savings clubs by telling them about the idea, and helping them set up a club.

When we looked at user-owned-and-managed clubs in the third chapter we discovered a thriving set of self-help devices distributed unevenly across geographical areas and among social groups. Would it not be a good idea to carry the idea of such clubs to poor districts, or to groups of poor people who are not yet familiar with them? Indeed, could we not go a stage further, and get actively involved in showing the poor how to set up and run such clubs?

Certainly, some governments and many non-government organizations active in development (the so-called NGOs) are now busy promoting savings clubs among the poor. From a slow start in the late 1970s their work has built up so that by now the number of members in such clubs runs into hundreds of thousands. In this part of the chapter we shall look at two large-scale efforts to do this, one in India, where NGOs are fond of setting up what they call 'Self Help Groups' (SHGs), and another, started in Latin America, where voluntary organizations promote 'Village Banks'. By spreading the

[1] The 'MicroCredit Summit' in February 1996.

idea of savings groups in this way NGOs are bringing the benefits of basic personal financial intermediation to many poor people, and sowing the seeds of its penetration into many more households.

The Indian 'Self Help Groups'

In many respects the savings groups that Indian NGOs promote are similar to 'Rabeya's fund', the ASCA type that we looked at in the second chapter. Typically, they have a membership of twelve to thirty. Their members are drawn from the same neighbourhood and meet regularly, sometimes weekly or fortnightly, but more often, monthly. At each meeting each member contributes a savings deposit: sometimes this is a fixed sum which is the same for each member and for each meeting, sometimes it varies. Usually members cannot withdraw their savings. As the fund builds up it is lent back to members, who repay according to a fixed periodic instalment plan or, sometimes, in a lump sum at the end of a term. In most SHGs interest is charged on the loans. Sometimes this income is ploughed back into the common fund, sometimes it is paid to members as interest on their savings, or as a 'dividend' (a share of the profits).

In other respects these NGO-promoted groups are rather different from the truly indigenous informal ASCAs. For one thing, many are composed only of women, whereas ordinary (unassisted) savings clubs, as we have seen, are often of mixed composition. Secondly, leadership of the group tends to revolve annually, with the Chair stepping down and a replacement being elected to take her place, whereas unassisted groups often have an informal manager who is unlikely to be changed during the lifetime of the group. Thirdly, the average level of interest charged on loans is lower than in unassisted groups. Fourthly, SHGs tend to have a number of objectives, of which turning savings into lump sums may not be the most important. Women's empowerment, poverty reduction, leadership development, 'awareness raising' (about issues deemed to be important for the poor), business growth, or even family planning or the development of group-based businesses may be seen as the main work of the group. This contrasts strongly with un-assisted groups (ASCAs and ROSCAs) who normally come together unambiguously to find a way of creating lump sums out of small deposits. Fifthly, the promoters may lend money to their SHGs or help and encourage them to take loans from banks, whereas

unassisted groups generally rely on their own money, using banks—
if at all—as a place to store excess funds. Finally, these SHGs
struggle to become permanent, whereas unassisted groups, as we
have seen, find many sound reasons to close their groups and start
new ones.

Promoter Preferences

What causes these differences? They can be attributed to the fact
that the aims of most promoters (and, crucially, their backers—the
donors) are not the same as those of most poor people who set up a
savings club. They are much more complex. Unassisted groups just
want to turn small sums into large ones in as quick and convenient
a way as possible. Promoter-NGOs have a much grander vision.
They are *development* organizations, and have come to SHGs from a
social development background, rather than from a financial service
perspective. So in reality it is not that they have said 'savings clubs
like ASCAs and ROSCAs are a good idea—let us spread the idea
around to other poor people'. They have said something more like
'we want to develop and empower the poor in many different ways:
these savings clubs may be a good way of getting the poor together
to work on that'. SHGs are sometimes described as 'entry points' to
social and political development.

This perspective explains the six differences between NGO-
promoted SHGs and unassisted groups that we listed above. Most
SHGs are composed of women because in the world of development
in the last twenty years it has come to be accepted that women have
been neglected by the 'development' process, and modern donors
and NGOs are making a determined attempt to reverse this. The
annually revolving leadership of SHGs can be attributed to the
development world's interest in 'leadership development'—the belief
that the poor may make gains if they can train leaders who can
press their case with officials and others who can influence their
lives. The lower interest rates reflect a widespread belief that
interest is inherently suspect, and high rates of interest exploitative.
This view is inherited from the old colonial preoccupation with
usury. The development industry is having a hard time coming to
terms with the power and usefulness of the judicious use of interest.
Many would rather not think about the problem, and in the
meantime are anxious to keep rates as low as possible. Several staff

members of promoting NGOs have said to me, 'if the SHG members are going to pay high rates of interest, they might just as well stick with the moneylenders and not form a group at all'. It is for them especially that I have tried to show, in Chapter Three, the importance and usefulness of a variable pricing mechanism in savings clubs.

Some but not all promoters are in favour of SHGs accessing external funds. But many who do lend to 'their' groups, or help the groups get access to bank funds, do so because of a mix of motives. In some cases promoters have simply underestimated the power of regular savings to build up capital. This may be compounded by an equally naïve underestimation of the poor's capacity to save. A story illustrates this. Several times I visited SHGs in lower-middle income areas of Indian towns and expressed surprise at the tiny amounts the members were saving. The accompanying officer from the NGO would say 'they are very poor—they can't afford to save more than Rs 20 a month'. But after some further investigation it emerged that almost all the members were also involved in informal ROSCAs or managed-chits, each putting in average sums of Rs 200 or more per month.

Some NGOs are keen on their members becoming involved in setting up new businesses, or expanding new ones, and they see access to external finance as an indispensable part of that process. If they have selected the group membership carefully, so that it really is a group of budding entrepreneurs, this may be a sensible course of action, though experience shows that it needs much careful nurturing. Other NGOs, taking a broader view, see linking SHGs to banks as part of an effort to bring the poor into the mainstream of India's financial life. The ambition is laudable, but whether it is best done through SHG-bank links is yet to be seen.

Long-Term Thinking

Perhaps the most striking difference between SHGs and unassisted groups is in their attitude to their life-span. Looking into this will help explain why it is that promoters favour a kind of ASCA as their model, and rarely help set up ROSCAs—ROSCAs being inherently time-bound. Because unassisted ASCAs are there just to swap a series of small pay-ins for a few big pay-outs, their members are quite happy to close them down when they no longer perform that role as effectively as available alternatives (which include closing the club down and starting new one). As time goes by, there are many reasons why closing down becomes a sensible course of action, as we saw in the third chapter. But SHGs (or their promoters) tend to have multiple goals, some of which require the SHG to stay around in the long term—permanently, if possible.

It is not just these goals that cause this preference for the permanent. It is also because of the way in which promoter help to SHGs is structured and paid for. An NGO and its donor have to make a considerable investment in setting up an SHG, an investment that is not rewarded, as an ordinary business is, with income. The fruits of SHG investment are measured in 'impact'— the degree to which women have become truly empowered, the degree to which their family incomes have risen and the extent to which their voice has become more influential in the home and in the community and so on. Measuring all this is not only very difficult but also a costly and time-consuming task, over and above the need to keep the SHGs running long enough to ensure that these ends are both met and measured. SHG-promoters are also under some pressure to demonstrate that their preferred form of financial services for the poor is as 'sustainable' as other modern alternatives, such as the 'providers' that we shall examine in the second part of this chapter. Indeed, 'sustainability' has become such a watchword of modern NGOs and their funders that it may be blinding them to the virtues of the transitory. If there is one thing that 'promoter NGOs' fret about more than anything else, it is that their savings groups will 'collapse' before certain goals are achieved, or once the NGO leaves them alone. Consultants are paid small fortunes to assess whether or not this will happen, and think up ways of ensuring that it does not happen.

SHG Federations

There are no known SHGs surviving in the long term after their promoting NGO has left them to their own devices. Aware of this, promoters have begun to learn what Credit Unions have learnt over the years—that in order for groups to overcome the factors that lead them to be short-lived, they need to be linked to some kind of higher body. The main functions of such a body are to provide:

- a secure home for surplus savings at a rate of interest normally better than that offered by the bank (often by lending the money

to another group in need of extra funds and willing to pay a good rate)
- additional loanable funds when needed (often by lending surpluses deposited with it by other clubs, but also by arranging loans from banks and other bodies)
- supervision so that disputes are controlled
- regulation to see that the rules are kept
- advice and training so that the clubs are professionally run at high standards
- a legal identity so that the clubs can enter into legally binding financial contracts with others
- the role of a spokesperson and advocate of savings groups
- protection of savings through insurance

In India, bodies that carry out these functions have become known as 'federations' of SHGs. A recent review (by the NGO, FWWB) of six of the leading federations shows how they are getting on.[2] Their objectives are broadly similar to the list given above. Most are formally registered with the government—unlike their constituent groups. They are young (the oldest is only six years old) and as yet small, having total membership of between 1,000 and 3,000. Despite this they are quite complex in structure, since most have three layers of organization—the primary group, a 'cluster' of local groups and then the federation itself. They are becoming professional, with most having full time paid staff. However, four of the six are still dependent on subsidies, mainly from donors via the NGOs that help set them up. Increasingly they recognize this as a weakness, and are trying to improve their financial management know-hows, not only to improve their own capacity to recover their costs but to strengthen themselves in their dealings with formal financial institutions. None of them are really the creations of their members—nearly all were, like the SHGs themselves, 'promoted' by NGOs, and only one of the six has broken free of its NGO chaperone and is operating independently. Like many of the SHGs, several of these federations have multiple aims, and engage in development work besides providing financial services. Whether this is wise is a question hotly debated by the federations themselves.

The Report provides a sobering picture of progress to date. It shows that promoters are still involved in the task of creating the

---

[2] See bibliography of this publication for details.

structures that will allow their dream—sustainable networks of permanent user-owned and user-managed ASCAs composed of poor women—to come true.

Village Banks

In India, the Self-Help Group movement arose gradually from the work and experience of many promoting NGOs. Another attempt at getting user-owned, group-based financial services going—the Village Banking movement—had very different origins. An original model was designed by a group of professionals in the field, the best known of whom is John Hatch.[3] The organization they formed, *FINCA*—the Foundation for International Community Assistance— published the model in 1989 in *Village Banking Manual*. As we shall see, the model incorporates several aspects of unassisted user-owned clubs like the ROSCAs and ASCAs described in Chapter Three, and is clearly based on an understanding of the dynamics of what I have called 'basic personal financial intermediation'. The model proved attractive to many NGOs and their donor supporters, who were seeking a system of community development through popular participation. Through these NGOs, Village Banking spread, initially throughout Latin America and then farther afield, especially in Africa. By the end of 1994 there were around 3,500 Village Banks serving more than 90,000 members (nearly all women) in more than 30 countries. They had savings balances exceeding three million dollars and outstanding loans of more than twice that figure.

We can place Village Banking somewhere in the middle of the promotion-provision continuum. Indian SHGs *always* start with savings, and some never access external funds. Even when they do access external funds the money might not come directly from the promoter, since the promoter's role may be to help the group get a bank loan. Village Banks, on the other hand, *always* start with the provision of an injection of cash from the NGO: this cash 'kicks off' the cycle of saving and borrowing that characterizes the system. Nevertheless the original promoters intended that their involvement with the Banks as financiers will be temporary, and their overall vision was the promotion of independent, self-financed and

---

[3] Other design pioneers working with Hatch in Bolivia in the 1980s were Robert Schofield and Achilles Lanao.

self-managed village-level institutions. It is because of this intention that I have chosen to discuss Village Banks in the 'promoters' half of the chapter.

The original Village Banking model as set out in the *Manual* is attractively neat and logical: it has the internal coherence and cyclical 'completeness' that makes the ROSCA so appealing. This is how it works.

A group of (say) thirty village women agree with their promoting NGO to start a Bank. The NGO starts the ball rolling by lending the Bank (say) $1,500, which is immediately shared out among the members so that each gets a loan of $50. The members agree to repay these loans to their Bank on a strict weekly instalment basis over sixteen weeks. With each weekly repayment they also make a fixed interest payment.

At the end of the sixteen weeks the Bank repays the whole amount with interest to the NGO. Village Bankers call this flow of cash from the NGO through the Bank to the members and then back through the Bank to the NGO, the 'external' account, since it has to do with the external funds that the Bank is handling. By repaying on time, the Bank is automatically eligible for a second loan, on similar terms and with a similar 16 week cycle.

However, from week one the Bank is also running an 'internal' account, which handles cash originating from its own members. One element of this is weekly savings, which each member makes in addition to her loan repayments. It is expected that over the sixteen weeks each member will save a sum equal to 20 per cent of her loan: in our case, this would be $10 per member, resulting in a total savings for the Bank of $300 during the first loan cycle.

The NGO recognizes and rewards this saving. It does this by increasing the size of the second loan by the amount saved. So the second loan will be $1,500 plus an extra $300 (also from NGO resources) for a total of $1,800, and each member will get a second loan of $60. Again she repays and again she saves 20 per cent of the value of her loan, so sixteen weeks later she has saved another $12 and her *third* loan will therefore be worth $72. The cycles continue, so that after seven cycles each member will have reached a loan size of $150. After seven cycles the NGO ends its involvement as a Bank financier, and the Bank continues on its own, using its accumulated 'internal' account to service its members' loan needs.

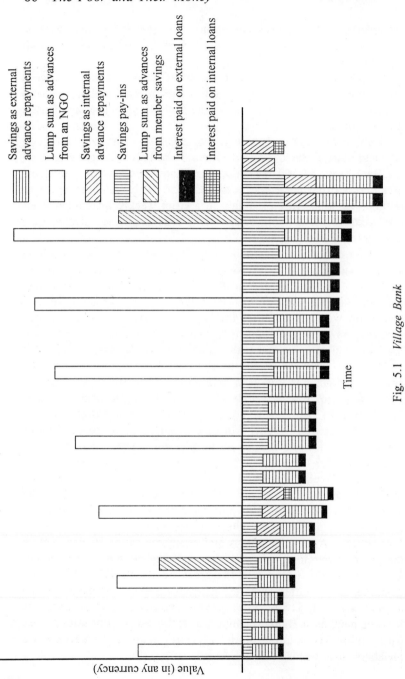

Fig. 5.1   *Village Bank*

This is deemed possible because the 'internal' account has not simply been accumulating savings. It has been revolving these savings in much the same way as ASCAs do—giving loans to members and agreeing repayment terms and interest rates. Moreover, since the Bank holds the repayments that members make on their 'external' account loans, and only hands them over to the NGO at the end of each cycle, the Bank also has that cash to use in its internal lending programme.

Figure 5.1 shows the regular progress of the seven external loans and their repayments, as well as the individually-tailored 'internal' loans that this particular member has taken. (For simplicity the diagram is presented in monthly rather than weekly intervals).

A notable feature of Village Banks that is clearly visible in the diagram is that the value of the loans rise steadily. This means that weekly repayments from members to their Bank (the amounts shown under the horizontal line in the diagram) also rise steadily in value through the external loan cycles. This illustrates an important assumption of the model—that loans will be invested in small businesses that quickly and continuously create the capacity to save larger and larger sums out of business profits. These are assumed to be mainly trading businesses. This is, therefore, not really a financial services model aiming at helping the poor turn a series of small sums into large sums. Rather it is a *small business promotion* model, aimed at helping the poor overcome poverty through assisted investment in business ventures. This is an important distinction that we can add to our list of differences between unassisted groups and promoted groups. We shall look at this difference again when we look at the new 'providers', in the second part of this chapter. Some of the providers also believe that the loans they sell should be invested in businesses, as opposed to satisfying any one of the large number of needs for lump sums of cash that we reviewed in the first chapter.

In its work as a *promoter*, the NGO that sets up a Village Bank is interested in promoting social and economic development goals—above all the participatory ownership and management of institutions by the poor and the development of poor-owned businesses. This combination of 'people power' and of business expansion has been the vision that more than any other has driven donors, NGOs and some governments in short, the development world of the 1990s. It is widely believed in such circles that this combination is the most promising, and perhaps the only route to effective poverty alleviation.

However, in its work as a *provider*, the NGO is interested in getting back the money it gives out as loans to the Banks. For this it depends primarily on 'peer pressure'. The second (and subsequent) loan is not disbursed until the first loan is repaid in full. So the Bank—a sort of collective of thirty women—has to be able not only to handle the collection and storage and use of the repayments it receives from members, but to enforce repayment. It can do this by warning bad payers that if they do not repay on time then the next external loan will be delayed, causing inconvenience to all the other members. If the 'shame' of this is not enough to persuade the recalcitrant member to pay up, the group can decide to expel her, or, sometimes, collect the money due by confiscating some of her goods.

This represents an articulated, specific threat based on the common-sense bargain that underlies all unassisted clubs such as ROSCAs or ASCAs. In those unassisted user-owned devices, it is obvious to all who take part that the thing will just not work unless everyone chips in as well as takes out. The risk of non-payment is well understood but is rarely articulated. But when, as in a Village Bank, 'external' funds are involved the bargain is less clear because *three* parties are now involved—the individual member, the club, and the NGO—and the relationship between them is not so obvious. It is not surprising that, three-way use of peer pressure has proved to be a problematic issue.

Ironically, it is not possible to make a direct comparison of the success rates in the use of peer pressure on unassisted and promoted groups. This is because the most common way that unassisted clubs tackle the problem is to close the club before the problem becomes severe, or to shun leaders or managers or members of clubs that have 'gone bad'. As we saw in our discussion of SHG attitudes to longevity, this simple but effective use of a 'survival of the fittest' policy is rarely available to SHGs and Village Banks. This is because their promoters, who have made considerable investments (not least of all, pride) in their promotees, and are reluctant to see them end.

Developments in Village Banking: Our description of the Village Bank was of the original model, as hatched in the 1980s. Since then, the model has been tried by new promoters in new situations, and many variations have come about, often in response to some of the issues we have been discussing in this chapter. This 'evolution' is healthy, and mimics the evolution that goes on all the time in the informal, unassisted sector, as we saw in the previous two chapters. The variations will not be reviewed here, but two trends can be noted because they help us push forward our story, and lead us into the section on providers.

In the original model the control and management of the Bank was unambiguously in the hands of its members, with the NGO acting as a guide, trainer and short-term financier. In many current versions of the scheme this clarity has disappeared. Finding that their Banks do not perform as well on their own as was hoped, many NGOs now take a much more active role in controlling the Banks. They have become, effectively, 'managers'—managing the Banks on behalf of their members. Indeed, I toyed with including a category of 'managers' in this chapter, since wherever I go find NGOs managing savings groups of one sort or other. However, most of these NGOs do not actively espouse the 'manager' role[4]: some prefer to believe that their groups will finally be able to manage their own affairs, given a little more encouragement, while others drift into the role of providers.

This drift into the provider role has occurred with many Village Bank promoters. Their role as financier to the Banks has proved not to be not just long-term, but in many cases even permanent. Indeed, the Village Banking movement as a whole is shifting away from the 'promoter' role and towards the 'provider' role. On a recent trip to East Africa, for example, I found that most MFIs using the Village Bank technology have dropped the idea of fostering independent user-owned institutions and now want to turn themselves into permanent providers of financial services to the poor. I asked one branch manager to tell me about the progress of the 'internal account'—the fund built from savings and owned by the members themselves, which is supposed to allow Bank members to become self-sufficient. The manager made it quite clear that while at one

---

[4] I have read that there are some NGOs (or MFIs) that manage ROSCAs or ASCAs but do not finance them. They take a fee for their management services, like chit-managers in India (Chapter Three), and intend to stay in the business long-term. I do not know how much success they've had, so I have not included them in this essay.

time her purpose had been to help members build up this fund and operate autonomously, her ambitions were now quite different. She now wants to maintain her branch as a permanent supplier of financial services to the members, and as such she sees the loans disbursed from the internal account as competition for the branch's own loan business. She told me, 'We would like to take over the loan business done by the internal fund.'

There are good reasons for this, which we now turn to.

THE PROVIDERS

There is of course a dilemma if one were at the 'promoter' end of the continuum. Getting together in a group to run their own savings and credit system may be a wonderful idea for the poor, but it has its costs. Someone has to do the book-keeping. Someone has to play the policeman, making sure everyone follows the rules. Time has to be given to meetings, to writing up resolution books as well as to do book-keeping. Even then, there is some risk that things will go wrong, and risk is another kind of cost. We saw all this in the third chapter.

There is an important lesson here. Poor people, in my observation on three continents, do not run savings clubs for the sake of it. They pay the costs of running a club because they value the services they get. *But if they could get an equally good service from someone else for less cost, they would prefer it.* It is true that ASCAs and ROSCAs show an astonishing propensity to survive even in environments where there are plenty of formal services, but that is because those formal services have yet to rival the flexibility and convenience of the home-made product.[5]

Promoters spend a lot of time setting up groups, training them, supervising them, fretting about them. This is despite—indeed this is often because of—the fact that the groups are supposed to do all their own management themselves. Is the time and effort put in by promoters worth it? The 'promoter' philosophy puzzles many group

---

[5] It is said that in modern Japan until very recently big businesses ran ROSCAs among themselves with contributions measured in millions of dollars, because it was easier and more convenient than dealing with Japan's inflexible and bureaucratic (and highly taxed) formal banks.

members, who rightly ask me 'if those nice people from the NGO are going to spend so much time on us why do *they* not do the management? After all, they are literate, we are not, they know how to manage finance, we do not: why do they insist that *we* do all this work?'

NGOs might have a good answer—'we are interested in community self-management, and leadership'—but group members might legitimately reply 'maybe, but we are interested in turning our savings into lump sums'. And when NGOs find themselves unable to shake off a share in managing the groups, and find themselves financing groups for the long term (as many Village Bank promoters are now doing) the question becomes unavoidable: 'would it not be more cost effective for us to run financial services *for* the poor rather than struggle to enable them to do so themselves?'

A Better Moneylender

With that we reach the world's most famous banker to the poor— the Grameen Bank of Bangladesh. Although the Grameen Bank sets up groups it is *not* a promoter. It does not try to get the group members to run their own services. Its groups are customer groups—a set of customers brought together at the same time in the same place each week to facilitate a loans service. The Grameen Bank owns the funds, and enjoys the income earned from the interest paid on loans.[6] Loans go to individuals directly from the bank, not from the group. Group members cross-guarantee each other's loans, but the group does not own the fund out of which the loans are made.

Grameen Bank is a provider. It provides a saving down service— that is advances against savings—to a mass market. From the user's point of view what Grameen Bank does is most similar to the urban moneylender we reviewed in Chapter Two. Figure 5.2 makes this clear.

---

[6] Grameen Bank is structured as a bank owned by share-holders. Every customer (group member) buys a share in the Bank and their representatives hold an overwhelming majority of seats on its Board. However in practice at the village level members are unaware of the implications of this and at the Head Quarter level, control is exercised *de facto* by the bank's professional management.

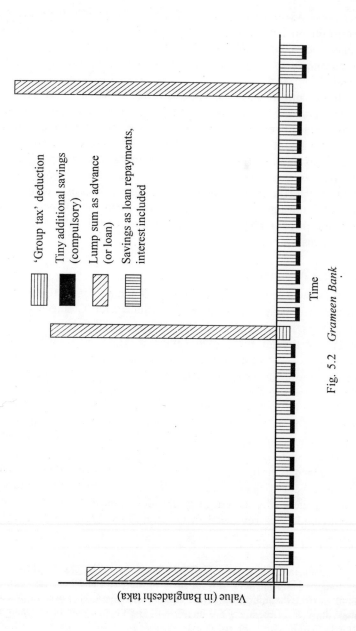

Fig. 5.2   *Grameen Bank*

Like the moneylender, Grameen offers a lump sum which is recovered in a series of small payments—in Grameen's case fifty weekly payments over one year. Like the moneylender, Grameen takes interest, but instead of deducting it at the time the loan is given, Grameen takes it in small easy-to-find instalments along with the repayments. As with the moneylender, most clients immediately embark on a fresh cycle as soon as one cycle is compete.

Grameen differs from the moneylender in some small respects and some important ones. Unlike the moneylender (at least the sort of urban moneylender we looked at in Chapter Two) Grameen does accept some savings deposits—in small regular fixed weekly instalments that cannot be withdrawn until the client has been in the system for ten years. It also deducts 5 per cent of the value of each loan for a 'group tax'—money that is put into a fund owned by the clients but held by the bank that can be used to bail out clients who get into trouble with their loans. This money too can eventually be claimed by the clients after ten years.

The big differences lie in Grameen's use of group-guarantees, the price of the Grameen Bank loan, the bank's reliability, and its scale. Like the Village Banks, Grameen insists that the clients which it gathers together in the weekly-meeting groups—normally about forty people—cross guarantee each other's loans. Moneylenders rarely use guarantees of any sort, let alone big group guarantees. They prefer to rely for good repayment on their personal knowledge of the client, on the mechanism of small-but-frequent instalments, and the client's dependence on them for future loans. The rate of interest charged by Grameen on advances is much less than the average moneylender's. Grameen charges a 'flat rate' of interest that is, a fixed sum each week. This is 10 per cent of the face value of the loan, but since the loan is paid off in weekly instalments the average value of the loan in the client's pocket is half the face value, so the interest rate on an APR basis (see Chapter Two) is twice the nominal rate: an APR of 20 per cent or about 1.66 per cent per month. The most frequent problem poor people face with moneylenders, however, is not the price but the availability—the poor find it hard to persuade someone to give them an advance. This is where Grameen really scores, because once a client is a 'member' of a weekly-meeting group she is guaranteed access to a series of advances, as long as she repays on time and her fellow-members do the same. To secure this rare right, Grameen clients struggle, sometimes at considerable cost, to maintain their repayments and retain their right to borrow. Moreover, the Grameen Bank differs from the moneylender in being a professional organization with a massive outreach. It had around two million clients (most of them village women) in the mid 1990s.

Finally, Grameen, again like the Village Bank promoters but unlike most moneylenders, tends to raise the value of the loan after each cycle. Dr Yunus, Grameen's brilliant founder and General Manager, believes that loans should be invested in starting or expanding businesses, and thus set off an upward spiral of investment and income, allowing the client to service ever-bigger loans. He is more interested in 'micro-enterprise finance' (loans to start and run small businesses) than in 'microfinance' (financial services for the poor) *per se*. Some clients do indeed start or expand businesses, but as we saw in Chapter One the needs for lump sums that the poor face are so numerous that all or even most of the lump sums can not put to business uses. Because of this, if Grameen has been active in a village for many years while loan values have risen to $200 dollars or more, many clients drop out altogether while others may experience repayment problems. We conclude that if you are swapping savings for a lump sum (given as an loan), the biggest lump sum you can handle must approximately equal your savings capacity for the term of the loan—unless the loan really is contributing directly and immediately to a rise in your capacity to save.

Promotion Versus Provision

Let us return to the question we posed at the end of the previous section. Is it worthwhile being a promoter? Well, if we measure the output of promotional work in terms of how much 'leadership' is created and how much participatory self-management is facilitated, then I have no idea—these things must be hard to measure and I do not know of any successful attempt to do so. But if we measure output in terms of the number of poor people receiving useful financial services, the verdict is clear: provision beats promotion hands down. The best place to see this is South Asia.

The Indian semi-formal sector has favoured the promotional stance. Over the years, large numbers of SHGs have been created. There are no wholly reliable counts, but we do know that the National Bank for Agricultural and Rural Development (NABARD), a government-owned institution may be helping around 100,000 group members by lending to such groups (through banks or NGOs). DFID (British aid) believes there may be around 75,000 NGO-sponsored SHGs altogether, with up to a million members, and a similar number set up by agencies of various sorts to take advantage of special loan schemes offered by central and state governments to such groups. In Bangladesh, a country with a similar poverty profile but one tenth the population, semi-formal financial services for the poor are dominated by providers. The Grameen Bank, alone probably has as many clients as the whole of the Indian SHG movement, and besides Grameen there are other giants—BRAC[7] and the Association for Social Advancement (ASA) with about 3 million and 1.5 million clients respectively each. Besides such figures, the world-wide outreach of Village Banks, which amounts to about 90,000 clients at the end of 1994, looks small.

There is no mystery about why the providers have been able to scale up faster. Since they control all the management of the financial service process, they can reap the benefits of scale if they make their management efficient. They don't have to wait around while a group of illiterate village women slowly learn how to distinguish income from liabilities. The signals that providers receive about their efficiency are much louder and clearer than those promoters get, because providers can offer a consistent service and watch what happens to it, while promoters find that each group tends to behave a little differently from the others. Providers can aim to cover their costs and generate a surplus, and thus work in a quasi-commercial or even fully-commercial market, something that doesn't apply to promotional work which is generally subsidised.

ASA: A Super-Charged Grameen

This market-like environment in which the provision of financial service to the poor operates in Bangladesh has had a visible impact on the development of institutions. In the mid 1970s Grameen was the originator of the standard Bangladesh product—the 'saving down' advance against a year's worth of weekly savings.

[7] BRAC was the acronymn for the Bangladesh Rural Advancement Committee but is now a registered name. It is a very large NGO in Bangladesh which also operates as a microfinance institution.

Latecomers have had the opportunity to learn from Grameen and do better. ASA came to microfinance in 1991, after a motley history as an NGO including, at one early point, a revolutionary stance in which armed ASA groups were to be trained to take political control of the country. When they replicated the Grameen product, they simplified its delivery by cutting out the five-person 'sub-groups' into which Grameen divides its 40-person client groups, and the delivery of advances became both quicker and more standardized. Meanwhile they adopted a much simpler organizational structure, cutting out the Area Offices and the Zonal Offices that stand between the Head Office and the branch in Grameen, and create their own paperwork and require extra staffing. Above all, ASA judiciously combines the *maximum* level of *delegation*, (so that lowly branch managers make the decision to disburse a loan without needing a signature from a higher officer), with the *minimum* level of *discretion* (the procedures are so cut and dried that it is hard for branch managers to make mistakes and equally hard to tempt them into rent-seeking).

Ever Better Providers

The providers may beat the promoters when it comes to the number of poor people they reach, but they have not won all the arguments. Promoters correctly point out that the standard Bangladesh Grameen-style product is rather inflexible: users get just one advance a year and are allowed only one way to repay it. This is not very user-friendly—it does not allow for other ways to make the 'basic personal financial intermediation' swap, such as saving up and withdrawing, and it does not help people who need small loans, several times a year, to meet their consumption needs. Nor is it convenient for long-term or insurance needs, such as providing for marriage or burial expenses. Finally, the insistence on using loans solely for business purposes is unrealistic, they claim.

Very recently—from about 1995 on—Bangladesh's big providers have begun to respond to these criticisms. We shall use the case of ASA to illustrate this. ASA has made a series of four modifications to its products.

First, ASA moved from 'compulsory' to 'voluntary' savings. As we have seen, in the standard Bangladesh model as pioneered by Grameen, clients are required to save rather modest amounts each week but enjoy very little access to the cash. In ASA's case up to 1997, they could not take their savings out until they left the scheme for good. Such blocked savings are known as 'compulsory' savings and were regarded by most ASA clients as simply a further cost of, or tax on, the advances they took. When ASA took the bold step of telling clients that they could have unrestricted access to their savings, clients withdrew massive amounts, to see whether this promise was going to be honoured. It was, and this increased client confidence in ASA so that savings began to flow back into ASA in ever larger sums.

Convinced that the poor *can* save in larger amounts than was previously thought (see Chapter One) ASAs next opened up a savings bank service to not just those who were already members of an ASA group but to everyone in the village. These 'non-group savers' have no right to take an advance: they are offered only a simple open-access savings account. They can save up but not save down. This too proved popular, with many friends and relatives of group members taking this rare chance of a secure home for their savings.

In May 1998 ASA went a step further. It introduced a 'con-tractual' savings product. We have seen contractual savings at work in the marriage funds described in Chapter Four. In ASA's case, clients contract to save a fixed sum each month for five years. If they succeed in doing so, they get back the whole of their savings plus profits at the end of the five-year term. Such schemes had long been offered by formal banks and were popular among middle and upper income people in Bangladesh, but ASA has become the largest provider to offer them to the poor.[8] Within four months over 200,000 accounts had been opened.

The combination of a standardized advance with an open access savings account and a contractual savings scheme is very attractive to the poor. It answers many of the criticisms made of the 'provider' model. This is shown in Figure 5.3.

This looks good, but can still be criticized. Before we go on to do that we must mention ASA's fourth innovation. Like most other Bangladesh providers, ASA initially insisted that all loans be used

---

[8] But it was not the pioneer. The honour probably belongs to the Social Development Society (SDS), a little-known NGO working in central Bangladesh. I found them offering this product to poor villagers way back in 1993.

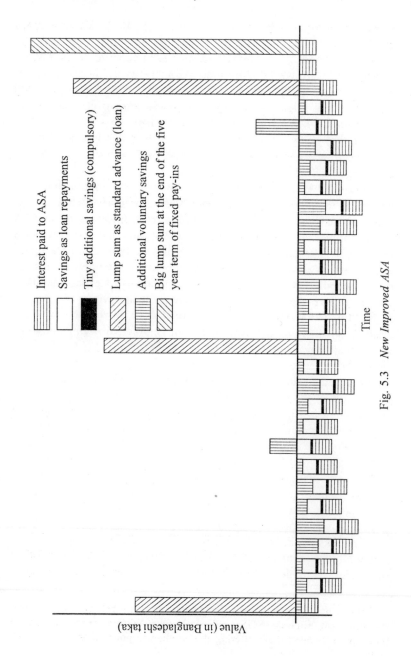

Fig. 5.3   *New Improved ASA*

for business purposes. But ASA came to see that the poor have many other needs for lump sums, and an advance that has to be repaid within a year starting the next week is not a financial instrument fine-tuned for business investment, to say the least. The internal rate of return that needs to be made by a business capitalized in such a way is frighteningly high. Moreover, with loans still small relative to the costs of setting up a 'real' business, as opposed to carrying on with the supplementary livelihood activities that the poor ordinarily engage in, like raising chickens or goats or cleaning paddy, it was clear that bigger loans would be needed. This is what ASA has done, and it is into this venture that much of the capital raised by the contractual savings scheme is going. However, here ASA is less adventurous than some other providers who are experimenting with a range of new business loans for 'real' entrepreneurs. Grameen itself has started a 'hire-purchase' system for capital goods for business people, and the microfinance institution BURO,[9] Tangail is experimenting with several different ways to reach and support small businesses. In other countries, notably in South America, research into the best way of supporting businesses is even further advanced.

Gono Bima: Life Insurance for the Poor

ASA's judicious mixture of short and long-term savings products alongside its loans provides its customers with a range of convenient and useful services. However, it has yet to offer specialized insurance products. Although ASA clients can use the long term savings scheme to build up some protection against financial problems they are likely to face in the future, many may still feel the need for protection against particular contingencies. That is why many of them are also customers of Gono Bima, a life insurance scheme for the poor.

Gono Bima (which simply means People's Insurance in Bengali) presents us with a number of novelties. Gono Bima is a subsidiary of a large private insurance company, and is therefore a good example of a recent phenomenon—the entry of formal financial institutions into the business of microfinance. Gono Bima is also set to be one of the first microfinance schemes with insurance, using

---

[9] BURO was the acronym for the Bangladesh Unemployed Rehabilitation Organization but is now a registered name.

true pooling rather than loans, as its core product. Here is how it works:

A very simplified and highly standardized life insurance scheme is marketed in the slums and villages from modest branch offices similar to those of ASA. To buy the insurance you need not undergo any medical test nor fill up complicated forms. The tiny premium is paid weekly or monthly, and the benefits are standardized. You pay in each week for ten years and at the end of that term you get your money back with profits. In the meantime, should the person named in the insurance cover die, you get the full amount just as if you had been saving for ten years. Gono Bima does not bring the income from insurance premium to its Dhaka headquarters. Rather, it circulates it back to its clients in small loans modelled on Grameen's basic product. The clients, therefore, get life insurance plus access to further advances when they need them. Figure 5.4 will help to illustrate the scheme.

You can see the close family resemblance to the Marriage Funds of Kerala shown in the last chapter. Gono Bima represents an early example of a formal institution picking up and marketing to the masses, a scheme that had previously reached the poor of South Asia in a small way through informal managers.

Back to SafeSave

What could be better for the poor than ASA's full set of services plus a life insurance policy from Gono Bima? To answer that we need to think about the *very* poor and go back to what was said about *Safe*Save at the end of the second chapter.

ASA's core product remains the standard advance. Two features of that product make it inhospitable for the very poor. The first is that the term is fixed: you can do it only once a year, and even the question of *when* you do it may not be under your control. This is because the timing of your first advance may have been determined by the date on which the ASA came and set up a group in your village, something that has nothing to do with your real needs.

But a more serious drawback is that the product requires fixed equal weekly repayments, and as we saw in the first chapter many poor people lack either the means or the confidence to do this. For that reason many 'exclude themselves' from membership, reluctantly letting an otherwise excellent opportunity escape.

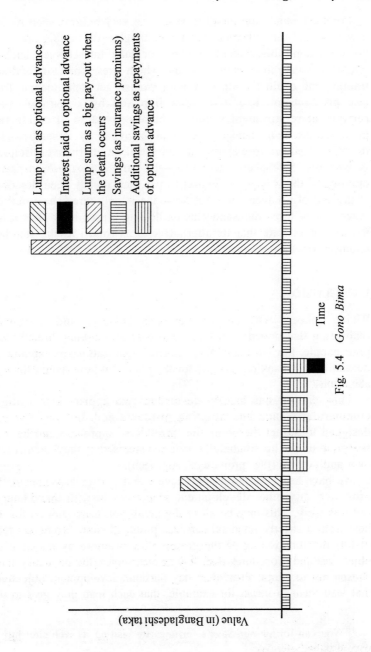

Fig. 5.4 *Gono Bima*

Products which are aimed to reach the very poorest need to find a way around this dilemma. So far in Bangladesh, the big providers have not done this, except in some special pilot schemes, such as BRAC's 'vulnerable group' scheme which uses a mix of food-aid, training and credit to help very poor women get some income from egg production. The *discipline* imposed by a regular fixed repayment requirement seems to have proved so effective that providers are understandably reluctant to give it up. It has been left to smaller players to experiment and see if an alternative discipline is available. *Safe*Save's alternative—the daily *opportunity* to pay as opposed to the weekly *obligation* to pay, has already been described at the end of Chapter Two. But *Safe*Save is only three years old and reaches only three thousand clients: despite a promising start it has yet to demonstrate that its alternative is as robust as the standard Grameen or ASA product.[10]

CONCLUSION

Rising concern with continuing world poverty, and a growing realization that poverty must be addressed by working directly with poor people, has led many development organizations to explore the possibilities of banking services for the poor. But how should they go about this?

This chapter has briefly described two approaches: using a commercial stance but adopting products and delivery systems designed to attract the poor (the 'providers' approach) and helping the poor to set up financial service systems that they themselves own and control (the 'promoters' approach).

We have seen that both approaches, and particularly that of the promoter, mix other development objectives in with the financial services work. This may be all to the good, but it may not be for the best from a strictly financial services point of view. Promoters may distort the functioning of the groups they promote by insisting on objectives and procedures that, left to themselves, the poor may have chosen not to adopt. Providers may harbour development objectives that lead them to insist, for example, that each loan they give to the

---

[10] You can follow *Safe*Save's fortunes by visiting its web site: http://www.drik.net/safesave.

poor must be invested in businesses—an unreasonable and unrealistic condition.

A better understanding of how the poor wish to manage their money, and a shift in emphasis from a concern with general development objectives to a sharper focus on improving the financial services might mean that many more poor people could get improved help to manage their money. The final chapter contains further observations of this sort.

6

Better Financial Services for the Poor

Creating better financial services for the poor starts with having a clear idea of just what constitutes good services. The good services enable the poor to swap frequently saved small sums of varied value into a lump sum when required in a quick, affordable and transparent manner.

The message of this essay is that financial services for the poor help them swap their savings for lump sums of cash. It follows that *good* financial services for the poor are those that perform this swap well. This requires:

- Products that suit the poor's capacity to save and their needs for lump sums so that they can
  - save (or repay) in small sums, of varied value, as frequently as possible
  - access the lump sums (through withdrawals or loans) when they need them for instance in the short term for some consumption and emergency needs, in the medium term for investment opportunities and some recurrent life-cycle needs, and in the longer term for other life-cycle needs like marriage, health-care, education and old age
- Product delivery systems, convenient for the poor that are
  - local, frequent, affordable and quick
  - not burdened with paperwork and other transaction costs
  - transparent in a way that is easy for illiterate people to grasp

It is not often that the short, medium and long-term needs for lump sums can be delivered within one product, although *Safe*Save, described at the end of Chapter Two, is an attempt to do just that. Usually, a range of products will be required. In slums and villages where informal financial services for the poor are well established, it is not uncommon for the poor to have a stake in several different schemes at once. In southern India, for example, they might be paying two rupees a week into a burial fund to secure their funeral, ten rupees a week into marriage funds for their sons or daughters, and two hundred rupees a month into a ROSCA (a chit fund) to assemble funds for a new roof. At the same time they may belong to a neighbourhood savings group where they can get fifty or hundred rupees quickly if they need it for some small household emergency. For a lump sum at even shorter notice they might use the pawn-broker. Intrigued by the newcomers in the financial services market, they may even have joined a Self Help Group set up by an NGO.

In areas where financial services for the poor have until recently been absent, rudimentary or unreliable, such as many parts of rural Bangladesh, a provider who offers a single product type, with only one kind of swap, may nevertheless be warmly welcomed. Grameen's simple one-year's-saving-advance, copied by hundreds of other NGOs in Bangladesh and elsewhere, was a brilliant innovation that has helped millions. However, as time passes, Grameen and its replicators have either modified their original product, or added more products to their range, or both, as we saw in the case of ASA (in the previous chapter). This careful development of a range of services, each building on the insti-tution's growing experience, is a sound policy.

The problem of the design of financial products for the poor is touched upon at the end of this chapter. First, though, we need to take another quick look at the institutions that deliver the services.

INSTITUTIONAL PROMOTERS

Although this essay is not, essentially, about institutions, our recapitulation of what constitutes good financial services for poor people would not be complete without some further reference to the 'promoters' and 'providers' whose work we described in Chapter Five. In fact, we need to add *two* further ingredients to our recipe for improved financial services for the poors:

- Institutions adapted to delivering good products that are:
  - committed to serving the poor; and
  - cost-effective
- A healthy environment for financial services for the poor including:
  - stable macro-economic and financial management by the government

- the rule of law
- helpful rather than restrictive legislation governing promoters and providers of financial services for the poor

Nothing more will be said about the environment. Nor will this essay attempt to discuss the vast subject of the design and management of financial service institutions that serve the poor. There are already many good texts and courses, some of which I have listed in the bibliography. What follows is a set of general remarks about the relationship between the types of institutions mentioned in Chapter Five and the kinds of products that best suit them.

Promoters with Mixed Goals

Where promoters have mixed goals this will affect the kind of financial service work that they can promote. For such institutions the main goals may be to develop social skills among the poor—participatory management, leadership, solidarity, business acumen and so on—and savings-and-credit schemes may be seen primarily as 'entry point' strategies, devices to lure the poor towards other activities that become attractive after some time. Commonly, this work is done in a group context, and offers the opportunity to promote group-based savings schemes. However, such promoters usually want to 'phase out' after a given period.

The financial service activities of such groups should be chosen with these conditions in mind. For example, schemes like the Annual Savings Club described in Chapter Four, or a two-year or three-year version of the same device, would be appropriate. From the pro-moter's point of view, such clubs offer a vehicle through which social and management skills can be transferred to the poor. With the promoter acting as supervisor the risk of things going wrong should be low. These clubs are time-bound, thereby relieving everyone of anxiety about 'what will happen when the promoter phases out?' From the group members' point of view, they will have the satisfaction of seeing a scheme mature and bear fruit, as they take home their savings-plus-profits at the end of three years, while in the meantime they have had at their disposal a savings and loan service of a type that most poor people find useful. A few may use this experience to set up, manage or merely join similar schemes in their slum or village after 'phase-out'.

Not all 'social development' NGOs believe that they should 'phase out' after a certain period. Some set up permanent branches at the slum or village level. These NGOs are placed well in order to foster user-owned schemes that have the potential of becoming long-lasting or permanent user-owned and managed institutions like the Credit Union (see the previous chapter and the next section below). They may also (or alternatively) become 'managers' (in the sense used in Chapter Four) and run long-cycle schemes for their members on a non-profit basis, such as marriage or burial funds, or multi-cycle ASCs or even ROSCAs. Or, of course, they may develop (as far as financial services work is concerned) into permanent 'providers' as the Bangladesh NGO Proshika has done over the last few years. The stresses of mixing social development work with financial service provision are, however, considerable, and NGOs wishing to go down that line would be well advised to study the experience of path-breakers like Proshika.

Promoters Who Focus on Financial Services

Though rare, there are promoters who are single-mindedly interested in promoting financial services for the poor, with no social aims other than the desire to see the poor managing their money better. In theory, they too need to make a crucial decision— are they going to promote time-bound devices like ROSCAs and annual clubs or do they wish to help the poor set up *permanent* financial services institutions? In practice, I know of few promoters who concentrate on time-bound devices.

That leaves those promoters who aim to set up permanent poor-owned poor-managed institutions. The first advice for them is 'if you have not already done so, get in touch with the Credit Union movement' (see the bibliography for addresses). Credit Unions have over 125 years experience of setting up and maintaining user-owned financial institutions.

These promoters should banish from their minds any idea of setting up a few groups, training them, and moving on to the next place. In both Chapter Three and Chapter Four I have examined the very good reasons why unsupported groups are very unlikely to survive in the long run. It makes much more sense for such groups to adopt a 'close-down-and-start-again' strategy.

The reasons for this will not be rehearsed again. Rather, let us draw out the consequences for promoters. The overwhelmingly important one is that promoters should be aware that they will be promoting not just groups, but, sooner or later, a secondary-level supervisory support body as well. That body can be a pre-existing one, but often no such institution exists or, where it does exist, may not have the capacity to take on the new groups, or may have become corrupt or inefficient or unresponsive. This leaves two options, one, bottom-up and the other, top-down.

The *bottom-up approach* depends on the promoter's ability to help group members build their own secondary body composed of people chosen from their own memberships and informed by their own experiences. Some Indian 'federations' are following this path, as we have seen in the previous chapter. But this is hard work, and as we saw in that discussion of India's experience, it is slow work, too. There are no conclusive success stories yet, though they may emerge in the next few years.

The other option is to develop a permanent secondary body that is not owned by the groups but provides services to them and pays its own way out of charges levied for the services. This approach is particularly appropriate for organizations situated midway on the continuum that stretches from promoters to providers. Where a promoter has been setting up groups and making loans to them, it should be able to bow out safely by leaving behind a reduced version of itself, staffed by professionals. Such bodies take over the promoter's funds so that they may continue to lend out to the groups. By charging for this, and selling to the groups other financial services such as insurance and deposit facilities, these bodies can cover their own costs. Only those groups which agree to accept supervision and advice from the body (and perhaps pay an annual fee) would be eligible to access these services.

Providers

Unlike promoters, providers face no general limitations on the kinds of products they can offer. Their task is threefold.

- They must develop the right products that is, those that are in demand by their prospective clientele.
- They must design a delivery system that ensures that the product reaches the poor.
- They must control their costs so that they can deliver the services at prices that their clients are willing to pay but which allow them to cover all their costs.

The second and third of these tasks—how to make sure you are really reaching the poor and how to reconcile this process with full cost-recovery—have sparked the fiercest debates and driven some of the finest innovations in the field of financial services for the poor in the 1990s. The literature, training courses and workshops devoted to these intertwined issues have grown enormously, and even a summary would be far beyond the capacity of this essay. The bibliography provides pointers to some of the excellent texts that I happen to have read, and to some courses.

But the first of these three tasks—the development of the right financial *products*—has been the orphan of the research effort and is only now coming into its own. For every ten articles on whether the Grameen Bank is pushing people above the poverty line, or whether its members use contraceptives more often than non-members, whether they send their children to school more, or get beaten up less often by their husbands, you will find only one article asking basic questions about the design of Grameen's *products*. Questions like 'should there be other loan terms besides the one-year weekly-repayment term?'

The essay ends, therefore, where it started, among poor people in their villages and slums, looking at how we find out about their financial service requirements.

PRODUCT DESIGN

Good product design begins with knowing something about the prospective customers and their financial service preferences. The best way of assembling this knowledge is to find out what services are already available, and to ask people why they are using them, and what they like and dislike about them. It might seem that this can be followed up by asking people what *other* financial services they would like, but I have found that this is not a helpful question, mainly because the illiterate poor are often unaware of what those 'other services' might be.

A better way, in my experience, is to ask people how they manage circumstances that are amenable to financial service intervention. For example, in a village which has only short-term ROSCAs, you might ask people how they manage reserves for their old age, or where they go to get quick cash in small amounts for household emergencies. In the Philippines I was pottering about in villages that had a good Credit Union which gave loans for 'productive' uses but little else. When I asked the villagers what other financial services they would like they were unable to articulate anything. So, knowing that poor Filipinos are getting increasingly interested in education, I asked them how they financed school and college costs and quickly discovered that this was a matter of considerable anxiety for them. When I told them that I knew of a bank that ran a contractual savings scheme aimed at helping people save up in easy monthly deposits for school fees, I was bombarded with requests to 'bring that bank to our village', and several women tried to get me to accept their savings there and then.

Savings and Loans, Not Savings or Loans

In planning the product you wish to deliver, try to avoid sterile arguments about whether the poor need 'savings' or 'loans'. As I hope this essay has made clear, this is a false notion. It is much more helpful to think creatively about ways of collecting small sums (be they savings *or* repayments *or* insurance premiums) and then of ways of turning them into large sums (be they loans, *or* withdrawals from savings, *or* insurance pay-outs). The poor do not have a 'natural' preference for savings over loans, or vice versa—they have a need to turn small pay-ins into large take-outs. They will use the version of the three basic swaps (saving up, saving down, and saving through) which happens to be on offer, and if all three are on offer they will take whichever is most convenient for them at that moment for that particular need.

The terms of the offer made them will be an important factor in their decision. *Safe*Save has shown this. Where it has offered low rates of interest on savings but generous loan sizes with low interest, most clients have chosen to take loans. In other experiments where the rate paid on savings has been raised and the permitted loan sizes lowered and their prices hiked, far fewer clients take loans and more choose instead to save and withdraw. Again, the fact that almost every Grameen client is a borrower whereas most clients of the 'Unit Desas' of the Bank Rakyat Indonesia (a famous MFI in that country) are savers does *not* show that Bangladeshis have a greater propensity to borrow than Indonesians. It merely reflects differences in the products available to them.

Are the Terms Clear?

Whatever swap is being offered, its terms must be clear. It must be absolutely unambiguously clear to both parties—to the customer and to the staff involved in providing the service—what the deal is. The examples given in this essay demonstrate this. Mary's merry-go-round (Chapter Two) is exemplary: 15 daily pay-ins of 100 shillings equals one 1,500 shilling pay-out every fifteen days. Grameen's main product (Chapter Five) is crystal clear: an initial pay-out of 1,000 taka must be matched by 50 weekly payments of 22 taka, starting the next week. Both are first class products.

This apparently obvious point is surprisingly often overlooked. In more than one country I have been told by NGO staff that 'this group here are a 'good' group, but in that village over there they aren't saving regularly', or 'they aren't repaying nicely'. The NGO may advance all sorts of plausible reasons for this ('there was a flood last year') and some implausible ones ('they belong to another tribe and they have a bad reputation') without stumbling on the real one—that in the other village badly-trained workers had not explained the swap clearly to the clients. Poor villagers might put some savings into a scheme that they do not understand, just to please a patron, but they will not put in much until they are completely sure of when and how and in what quantities they can get their savings back, whether as withdrawals or as loans.

It is a good exercise to write out the rules of the scheme on one side of a sheet of paper. I am sometimes astonished by what happens when I ask NGOs to do this. Often, within minutes, the officers are quarrelling. 'Why have you written that clients can withdraw 25 per cent of their savings at any time?—they are only allowed to do that after two years of membership'. 'Oh really? I thought we'd agreed…' Having got it written out simply and clearly, (in the clients' language, of course) use this document as the basis for a flyer to be given to all clients, and for the purpose of staff training.

Delivery

When a decision is being made on the swap or swaps the institution wants to provide, the delivery mechanism has to be taken into account at the same time. It is not practical to separate these tasks. *Safe*Save's product, for example, depends on its ability to send collectors to each client each day: without that a key characteristic of the product, its use of frequency to maximize the rate of savings, would not work.

As we have seen, from the client's point of view good delivery means just one thing: a simple quick convenient means to make pay-ins and take pay-outs. How this will be done will depend on many factors, including, for example, the relative costs of labour, transport and machinery, and the density of population. In a low-wage economy like crowded Bangladesh *Safe*Save is able to employ staff who go daily, on foot, to the home or business of each client. In Panama, by contrast, there is a scheme that installs in slums ATMs (automatic teller machines) which both accept and pay out bank notes.

In both cases the agent doing the delivery (the staff member or the ATM) has been 'programmed' according to a precise set of rules, so that they have little or no discretion. As we saw when we looked at ASA, the secret behind its successful delivery is that it can be wholly and safely delegated to the field worker. This speeds up delivery, increases customer satisfaction and keeps it cheap. This is another reason why rules need to be unambiguous and clear.

Note that devices such as group formation, and 'social collateral' (group guarantees, sometimes called 'peer pressure' or 'joint liability') are best understood as optional components of a delivery strategy. A recent tendency to regard them as almost 'magical' ingredients without which banking with the poor is simply not possible should be resisted. Group formation is but one of many ways of organizing access by clients to the services on offer. Others include regular daily visits to individuals (as in *Safe*Save), fixed collection points that are attended at fixed times, and various kinds of agency arrangements. 'Social collateral' is in fact just one version of a large family of cross-guarantee systems. These in turn are simply members of an even bigger family of methods for reducing the lender's risk and include holding savings as security, taking personal references, and good old-fashioned collateral, as practised by pawnbrokers.

The Importance of Being Wise After the Event

As soon as the product starts being delivered the surprises begin. Assumptions are revealed. It had been supposed that clients would behave in a particular way—but they turn out to be doing something quite different.

This maybe because there are factors affecting their household economies, or merely the household cash-flow, that one was not aware of. It could be another financial service that you had not earlier discovered. In Pakistan I visited a competent and enthusiastic replication of Grameen but found that the villagers were not very interested in taking it up: the few that had been persuaded to join were not repaying their loans on time. A little time in the village revealed a very strong local ROSCA tradition that the organizers had not been aware of. It offered deals that many villagers viewed as superior to what the new provider had hoped to sell.

However, it could be that there is a seasonal effect that is stronger than one had anticipated. Maybe some cultural norm has been violated. This needs to be found out. Then, armed with such discoveries, one can go back to the drawing board and develop alternative products that serve another set of needs, or serve the same needs in an attractively novel way. As this essay has shown there is no shortage of ways to make swaps.

Here again we discover yet another reason for absolute clarity in the rules governing the product. Where rules are clear and have been fully and repeatedly explained to the clients, patterns of client behaviour will be sharp and evident. Economists would say 'market signals are loud and clear'. Where rules are not clear, client behaviour may differ according to each individual client's own distinct understanding of the rules (or each worker's individual interpretation of the rules). The lesson is, *clarity brings learning, and learning ushers in beneficial change.* Too many schemes suffer from the opposite: ambiguous products provoking confusing responses from clients and leading to protracted periods of poor performance.

CONCLUSION

In the Introduction I mentioned that a better *understanding* of financial services for the poor should lead to better *provision* of such services. The bulk of this essay—chapters one to four—has been an attempt to articulate what I have understood about financial services for the poor over the last twenty years. The later part of the essay—chapter five—discusses and critiques the exciting new wave of financial service provision that has been developing world-wide during those twenty years.

The opening pages of this chapter are as close as I am likely to get to an overall conclusion of my arguments. I summarize them in a final box:

Box 6.1   Financial Services for the Poor

Good financial services require:

* Products that suit the poor's capacity to save and their needs for lump sums so that they can
  - save (or repay) in small sums, of varied value, as frequently as possible
  - access the lump sums (through withdrawals or through loans) when they need them: in the short term for some consumption and emergency needs, in the medium term for investment opportunities and some recurrent life-cycle needs, and in the longer term for other life-cycle and insurance needs like marriage, health-care, education and old age

* Product delivery systems that are convenient for the poor and
  - are local, frequent, quick and affordable
  - are not burdened with paperwork and other transaction costs
  - are transparent in a way that is easy for illiterate people to grasp

* Institutions adapted to delivering good products that are
  - committed to serving the poor
  - cost-effective

* A healthy environment for financial services for the poor including
  - stable macro-economic and financial management by government
  - the rule of law
  - enabling rather than restrictive legislation governing promoters and providers of financial services for the poor

---

Suggested Reading

GENERAL

A handy (if sometimes irritating) way to keep up to date with *arguments about financial services for the poor* is to subscribe to DevFinance, an email chat service run from Ohio State University in the USA. Just send an email to listproc@lists.acs.ohio-state.edu and in the body of the message type SUBSCRIBE DEVFINANCE [your name]. The enterprising Hari Srinivas runs (from Tokyo) another electronic service, this time web-based, called The Virtual Library on Microcredit, to be found at www.soc.titech.ac.jp/icm/. It has sections in languages other than English. Malcolm Harper keeps a collection of informally published papers on microfinance at Alternative Finance, www.alternative.finance/org.

You can also subscribe to some *journals*. Free ones include those put out by the Consultative Group to Aid the Poorest (CGAP) which produces a newsletter, focus notes, and occasional papers. The CGAP is a sort of club of donors interested in financial services for the poor, housed at the World Bank in Washington (cgap@worldbank.org). Journals that regularly feature articles on financial services for the poor include *Savings and Development; World Development;* and *Small Enterprise Development.* Look for them at your library.

CHAPTER ONE

The *definition of poverty* has been hotly debated. Robert Chambers favours a view of poverty that takes into account many aspects other than financial and economic ones. See his *Poverty and Livelihoods: Whose Reality Counts?*, (1995, the Institute of Development Studies, Sussex University, UK). For practical purposes of distinguishing the poor from the non-poor Martin Greeley, also of IDS, favours the use of a 'poverty line' based on food consumption. He argues this in relation to financial services for the poor in an essay called 'Poverty and Well-being: Policies for Poverty Reduction and the Role of Credit' in *Who Needs Credit?*, edited by Wood and Sharif (1997, UPL, Dhaka and Zed Books, London).

The *definition of financial services for the poor* which I give in Chapter One first appeared in a piece I wrote for ACTIONAID and Oxfam and published by ACTIONAID as a working paper in 1996, called *A Critical Typology of Financial Services for the Poor.* This is a collection of (literally) fifty-seven varieties of financial services for the poor, each briefly described and commented on.

A good discussion on the *various types of financial services for the poor* can also be found in a collection of essays edited by Dale Adams and D. Fitchett called *Informal Finance in Low-Income Countries* (1992, Westview Press, Boulder, Colorado). It includes a piece by a pioneer of research into how poor people handle their money someone I greatly admire—Fritz Bouman.

Another good essay on the *poor and their money* is by Manfred Zeller, 'The Demand for Financial Services by Rural Households—Theory and Empirical Findings'. This was a paper presented in December 1993 at the Nordic Workshop on Rural Financial Services in Africa, in Harare.

I first elaborated the idea of *basic personal financial intermediation* in an essay I wrote with Sukhwinder Singh Arora of DFID (official British aid) in Delhi, called *City Savers*, in 1997. The essay deals with many of the same themes as this present work, but in the context of India, and specifically DFID's poverty-reduction work there.

An early essay stressing the importance of *savings* in financial services for the poor is the one by R Vogel, 'Savings Mobilization: The Forgotten Half of Rural Finance' in another work edited by Dale Adams, this time with J. D. von Pischke, called *Undermining Rural Development with Cheap Credit,* (1984, Westview Press, Boulder, Colorado). Adams was an important early critic of sub-sidised credit schemes.

CHAPTER TWO

For more details on West African *deposit collectors* see Douglas Graham's essay about Niger in the Adams book quoted above. For

Ghana see Ernest Aryeetey and Fritz Gockel, 'Mobilizing Domestic Resources for Capital Formation in Ghana', *African Economic Research Consortium, Research Paper 3,* Nairobi, August 1991.

For more on *interest rates* and how to set and calculate them see CGAP's Occasional Paper number 1 (see above under 'general' for details about CGAP). This particular paper was written by Rich Rosenberg.

Robert Christen wrote a piece called *What Microenterprise Credit Programs Can Learn from the Moneylenders* which records other aspects of *moneylenders.* It was published by Accion International in 1989 as their document 4.

Books and articles on *merry-go-rounds,* and other forms of *ROSCAs,* are given later, under the section for chapter three. One general recent book is *Money-Go-Rounds,* edited by Shirley Ardener and Sandra Burman, (1995, BERG, Oxford and Washington D.C.). It focuses on ROSCAs and women.

There is more on Dhaka's 'Funds' in my article in the Wood and Sharif (eds) book mentioned above.

Updates on *Safe*Save are available on its web-site, www.drik.net/safesave.

The need for women to save up for their *widowhood* is one of many topics well treated in Helen Todd's book on Grameen Bank, *Women at the Center,* (1996, UPL, Dhaka).

The *exclusion of the very poorest* as a consequence of fixed equal periodic pay-ins is dealt with in my article 'The Savings of the Poor', *Journal of International Development,* Vol. 10, No. 1, January 1998.

CHAPTER THREE

The original essay on *ROSCAs* by Shirley Adenar, called 'The Comparative Study of Rotating Credit Associations' was published in the 1964, *Journal of the Royal Anthropological Institute,* Vol. XCIV, London, but is reprinted in *Money-Go-Rounds,* referred to above. F.J.A. (Fritz) Bouman's essay, 'The ROSCA. Financial Technology of an Informal Savings and Credit Institution in Developing Countries' is another classic. It came out in *Savings and Development,* Vol. 3, 1979. A more recent article of his is 'Rotating and Accumulating Savings and Credit Associations: A

Development Perspective', *World Development,* Vol. 23, No. 3, 1995. Robert Christie has studied ROSCAs and is happy to correspond with others about them—his email address is R.Christie@isu.usyd.edu.au.

Surinder S. Jodhka's article, 'Who Borrows? Who Lends?' in the *Economic and Political Weekly,* September 30, 1995, pp. A-123–30 reports of instances of reciprocal obligation.

For the *Dhaka ROSCAs* see my essay 'Informal Financial Services in Dhaka's Slums' in *Who Needs Credit,* edited by Wood and Sharif, (1997, UPL, Dhaka and Zed Books, London).

For general background on *savings clubs* of all sorts in Bangladesh (which serves as a good introduction to the subject) there is *Rural Savings and Credit in Bangladesh* by Clarence Maloney and the late A B Sharfuddin Ahmed, (1988, UPL, Dhaka).

For more references to and examples of different kinds of savings groups see my *Critical Typology,* already mentioned above.

Warren Brow discusses insurance for the poor in a forthcoming paper for USAID, to be titled 'Insurance Provision in Low Income Communities'. Jean-Philippe Platteau's article is called 'Mutual Insurance as an Elusive Concept in Traditional Rural Communities', in the *Journal of Development Studies,* Vol. 33, No. 6, August 1997.

Informal Finance: Some Findings for Asia has a self-explanatory title. It is by Prabhu Ghate and others and published by Oxford University Press for the Asian Development Bank (ADB), 1992.

I have not seen any other write-up on the *ubbu-tungngul.* An unpublished report I wrote for the Central Cordillera Agricultural Program (CECAP), an EU-financed project based in Banaue discusses the *ubbu-tungngul.* They and the *initial investment funds* of The Philippines are discussed in.

CHAPTER FOUR

Marriage funds and *burial funds* were described by Sukhwinder Arora and me for DFID (British Aid) in an unpublished document written for them, *Almirahs Full of Passbooks* (February 1996, DFID Urban Poverty Group, Delhi).

The *Annual Savings Club* is described in more detail in *City Savers,* referred to earlier.

There is a huge literature on *Credit Unions.* Those interested in their history (beginning in nineteenth-century Europe) might like a new article by Hollis and Sweetman called 'Microcredit: What Can We Learn from the Past?', *World Development* Vol. 26, No. 105, 1998. Carlos Cuevas of the World Bank wrote an article for an edition of *Savings and Development* (No. 1 1988, XII) called 'Savings and Loan Co-operatives in Rural Areas of Developing Countries: Recent Performance and Potential'. A case-study of what is presented as a successful revitalization of a rural Credit Union system in Sri Lanka which works with the poor—Sanasa—can be found in the Hulme and Mosley book already mentioned, *Finance Against Poverty,* Vol. 2. Fritz Bouman's delightful book, *Small Short and Unsecured: Informal Rural Finance in India* (1989, Oxford University Press) is helpful because it describes Credit Unions (CUs) in the context of prevalent informal and semi-formal financial services in India, so the reader gets a feel of how the CU differs from other systems. The World Council of Credit Unions (WOCCU) is in Madison, Wisconsin USA (PO Box 2982, Madison, Wisconsin 53701-2982): they have publications.

I found a description of the work of the alajo (a Nigerian deposit collector) in an article in *Gemini News* headlined 'Alajos Growing Increasingly Popular as Community Banks in Nigeria' by Celestine Okonkwo.

The Vietnamese *moneylending couple* are written up in a series of unpublished reports that I wrote for ActionAid Vietnam over the period 1992 to 1997. They can be contacted on aav@netnam.org.vn.

Pawnbroking is well treated in an essay by Fritz Bouman and R. Bastiaanssen which appears in Chapter 13 of the book edited by Dale Adams and D. Fitchett, *Informal Finance in Low-Income Countries*, already mentioned. Fritz Bouman also discusses them in another book mentioned above, *Small Short and Unsecured.* The rates I quote for the various precious metals are derived, however, from my own research in southern India.

The *dadon (tied credit)* system for financing fresh-water prawn cultivation in Bangladesh is described in a report I wrote for the NGO CARE called 'CARE and Gher: Financing the Small Fry', unpublished 1994, CARE Bangladesh.

CHAPTER FIVE

A 1992 special edition of the journal *Search* (December 1992, Vol. VII, No. 4, Bangalore) looked at a large number of NGO schemes that promote *self-help groups (SHGs) in India.* FWWB (Friends of Woman's World Banking) is one such NGO and has issued a very short very clear handbook on their work methods, called *Organising Savings and Credit Groups for Poor Women* (1993, FWWB, Ahmedabad). Pradan, another NGO, has published *From Self-Help Groups to Community Banking* (1997, Pradan, Madurai). A third such NGO is Myrada: see *The Myrada Ex-perience* by their leader, Fernandez, Aloysius Prakash (1992). Outsiders writing on NGO work with SHGs include official Swiss Aid (SDC) in Delhi: they have written a new review in 1998.

FWWB has recently published a new paper on *federations of SHGs.* It is *India's Emerging Federations of Women's Savings and Credit Groups,* (March 1998, FWWB, Ahmedabad). The paper is discussed in the text of Chapter 3.

Malcolm Harper (with others) has recently written an up-beat book on the virtues of *self-help groups.* It is called *The New Middlewomen: Profitable Banking Through On-Lending Groups* (1998, Oxford and IBH Publishing Co. Pvt. Ltd., New Delhi).

The section on the origins of *Village Banks* relies heavily on a review by Candace Nelson, Barbara MkNelly, Kathleen Stack, and Lawrence Yanovitch called *Village Banking: The State of the Practice,* (1995, SEEP, New York). The notes on current developments in Village Banking relies on visits I made to the MFIs FINCA and PRIDE in East Africa in the spring of 1999.

As the world's most famous microfinance institution, the *Grameen Bank* of Bangladesh has been the subject of many books, studies and articles. I recommend the new reader to begin with just two. Grameen Bank was founded by Muhammad Yunus, and his early essay, called *The Grameen Bank Project in Bangladesh* (1982, Grameen Bank, Dhaka), remains one of the clearest statements about the aims and methods of the Bank. The best written and most illuminating recent book on Grameen is by Helen Todd and is called *Women at the Center* (1996, UPL, Dhaka).

There is nothing substantial yet published on *Gono Bima.*

For (ASA) I would immodestly recommend my own book, *ASA, the Biography of an NGO* (1995, ASA, Dhaka), because it tells the story of ASA, describes the products and delivery methods, and includes material on financial services for the poor in general, and on the Bangladesh context in particular. ASA itself regularly produces material. Practitioners might like *ASA, experience in action*, by Kurt Healey (1998, ASA, Dhaka), which is up-to-date describes the systems in full detail, including translations into English of all management forms and documents. Kurt has also written *ASA: Innovations in Informal Finance* (1999, ASA, Dhaka). Other titles can be had by emailing ASA on ASA@bd.drik.net.

A good review of the work of *Bank Rakyat Indonesia (BRI)* is *Progress with Profits, The Development of Rural Banking in Indonesia*, by Richard H Patten and Jay K. Rosengard (1991, Institute for Contemporary Studies (ICS), San Frencisco, USA).

For *Proshika's work in financial services,* there is a series of unpublished reports for Proshika by their financial services consultant, Lorna Grace.

CHAPTER SIX

There are now many good books and articles on *the design, development and management of financial service providers (i.e. microfinance institutions or MFIs) to the poor.* A good up-to-date text book is Robert Peck Christen's *Banking Services for the Poor: Managing for Financial Success,* February 1997. Christen runs a 'Microfinance Training Course' each summer at the Economics Institute in Boulder, Colorado, which is regarded as the premier course in MFI management. USAID, a major donor in the financial services field, has been running, since 1996, an ongoing project called 'Microfinance Standards'. CGAP, already mentioned above, devotes many of its publications to improved microfinance management. For organizations that are specifically interested in using financial services to promote small businesses there is *An Institutional Guide for Enterprise Development Organizations*, edited by Elaine Edgcomb and James Cawley (1993, SEEP, New York). Hartmund Schneifer has edited a book for the International Fund for Agricultural Development (IFAD) called *Microfinance for the Poor?* (with the OECD, 1997) which brings together essays on designing and developing MFIs and on interesting self-managed schemes from around the world, by several good authors.

The Economics Institute in Boulder Colorado puts out a *Microbanking Bulletin* which reviews the performance of selected MFIs.